INTERRUPTING SILENCE

Also by Walter Brueggemann
from Westminster John Knox Press

Abiding Astonishment: Psalms, Modernity, and the Making of History
(Literary Currents in Biblical Interpretation series)
Cadences of Hope: Preaching among Exiles
Celebrating Abundance: Devotions for Advent
Chosen? Reading the Bible amid the Israeli-Palestinian Conflict
The Collected Sermons of Walter Brueggemann, Volumes 1 and 2
First and Second Samuel (Interpretation series)
From Whom No Secrets Are Hid: Introducing the Psalms
Genesis (Interpretation series)
Gift and Task: A Year of Daily Readings and Reflections
Great Prayers of the Old Testament
Hope for the World: Mission in a Global Context
Hope within History
*An Introduction to the Old Testament: The Canon and Christian
Imagination, Second Edition* (with Tod A. Linafelt)
Isaiah 1–39 (Westminster Bible Companion series)
Isaiah 40–66 (Westminster Bible Companion series)
Journey to the Common Good
Living Countertestimony: Conversations with Walter Brueggemann (with
Carolyn J. Sharp)
Mandate to Difference: An Invitation to the Contemporary Church
Many Voices, One God: Being Faithful in a Pluralistic World (with
George W. Stroup)
Power, Providence, and Personality: Biblical Insight into Life and Ministry
Reverberations of Faith: A Theological Handbook of Old Testament Themes
Sabbath as Resistance: New Edition with Study Guide
Struggling with Scripture (with Brian K. Blount and William C.
Placher)
Texts for Preaching: A Lectionary Commentary (with Charles B. Cousar,
Beverly Roberts Gaventa, J. Clinton McCann, and James D.
Newsome)
Truth Speaks to Power: The Countercultural Nature of Scripture
Using God's Resources Wisely: Isaiah and Urban Possibility
The Vitality of Old Testament Traditions, Second Edition (with Hans
Walter Wolff)
A Way Other than Our Own: Devotions for Lent (compiled by Richard
Floyd)

INTERRUPTING SILENCE

God's Command
to Speak Out

WALTER BRUEGGEMANN

WESTMINSTER
JOHN KNOX PRESS
LOUISVILLE · KENTUCKY

First edition
Published by Westminster John Knox Press
Louisville, Kentucky

18 19 20 21 22 23 24 25 26 27—10 9 8 7 6 5 4 3 2 1

Book design by Erika Lundbom-Krift
Cover design by Mark Abrams

Library of Congress Cataloging-in-Publication Data
Names: Brueggemann, Walter, author.
Title: Interrupting silence : God's command to speak out / Walter Brueggemann.
Description: Louisville, KY : Westminster John Knox Press, 2017. |
  Identifiers: LCCN 2017047327 (print) | LCCN 2017048884 (ebook) | ISBN
  9781611648508 (ebk.) | ISBN 9780664263591 (pbk. : alk. paper)
Subjects: LCSH: Silence--Religious aspects--Christianity. |
  Silence--Religious aspects--Christianity--Biblical teaching.
Classification: LCC BV5068.S55 (ebook) | LCC BV5068.S55 B78 2017 (print) |
  DDC 248.4--dc23
LC record available at https://lccn.loc.gov/2017047327

Most Westminster John Knox Press books are available at special quantity discounts when purchased in bulk by corporations, organizations, and special-interest groups. For more information, please e-mail SpecialSales@wjkbooks.com.

For
Rolf Jacobson
Carolyn Sharp
Brent Strawn
Christine Yoder

I am pleased to dedicate this book to my friends Rolf Jacobson, Carolyn Sharp, Brent Strawn, and Christine Yoder. They are among the most important voices in a younger generation of Old Testament scholars. They have been generous in giving me access to their work, their methods, and their thinking that runs well beyond my old-fashioned ways. I am grateful for their work and their friendship.

CONTENTS

ACKNOWLEDGMENTS

I AM GLAD TO THANK THE USUAL SUSPECTS FOR BRINGING this little book to completion. David Maxwell first suggested it to me and did heavy lifting to bring it to fruition. The good folk at Westminster John Knox, notably Julie Tonini, have done their usual careful, patient work, and I am grateful.

Beyond these immediacies, I am grateful to the good company of companions who have not only taught me the urgency of breaking the silence but have stood by me through the process of breaking my own silence. That includes a host of teachers, colleagues, and pastoral companions, among them most especially Gerald Jenkins, who saw beyond my silences. Of course our silence breaking is deeply rooted in the biblical tradition of coming to speech, most notably the Hebrew slaves who refused the silence of Pharaoh. Those silence breakers, however, were only an echo of the God who broke the silence of chaos with a command to the light.

We now live in a barbaric world where the stones cry out against the violence that spirals from the top down. Our work is to join their refusal of silence and their brave insistence on voice.

INTRODUCTION

SILENCE IS A COMPLEX MATTER. IT CAN REFER TO AWE before unutterable holiness, but it can also refer to coercion where some voices are silenced in the interest of control by the dominant voices. It is that latter silence that is the primary focus of the studies that follow.

On April 15, 1967, at Riverside Church in New York City, Martin Luther King Jr. gave an address to Clergy and Laymen Concerned about Vietnam titled "Beyond Vietnam: A Time to Break the Silence." In that address, King not only spoke vigorously against the U.S. war policy in Vietnam, but he also linked opposition to the war to the crisis of race that he had long addressed. I remember that address; like many others at the time, I feared that in linking the war to the racial crisis King was detracting focus and energy away from the race crisis. But, of course, I, along with many others, was wrong. King understood that the war and race belonged to a cluster of issues, all of which flow together in a collusive silence in which public opinion had silently accepted top-down authority. King's breaking of the silence was a freighted moment in mobilizing sustainable opposition to the war in a challenge to settled authority.

King's capacity to break the silence that supported the war is representative of many movements that break the silence of long-protected practices of domination and exploitation. Most recently a number of church bodies have begun, albeit belatedly, to speak out against the church's pernicious, still-in-effect "Doctrine of Discovery" that long ago (and until now) cedes "the new world" to the old European colonizing powers, a ceding that currently feeds white nationalist sentiment in the United States. Such belated protests that work toward abrogation of that long-standing "doctrine" have come with an awareness that we must not be silent. In fact, many groups are now insisting that we must not be silent any longer, such as many liberation movements, among them feminism and womanism in many varieties, queer theology, Black Lives Matter, and voices of and for the disabled. In the Bible, perhaps the most vigorous character in such silence breaking is the importunate (nagging!) widow in Jesus' parable in Luke 18:1–8. All of these silence breakers have come to see that silence is a strategy for the maintenance of the status quo, with its unbearable distribution of power and wealth. Silence breakers characteristically insist that the old patterns of power must be disrupted and reconfigured. Thus the widow asked for and insisted on justice.

The silencers variously intend to maintain the status quo. In the ancient text the paradigmatic silencer is above all Pharaoh, a metaphor for all silencers, a company that comes to include, in the biblical tradition, kings, priests, scribes, and "the crowd" that was uncritically allied with such powers. We know very well in our time, moreover, that many voices are required for the maintenance of a democracy, and so the silencers resort to voter repression and gerrymandering, strategies for silencing those who would disrupt present power arrangements.

Thus, the ongoing historical process can be seen as an unequal contest between the silencers and those who would break the silence in the interest of new historical possibility. The contest is unequal because the silencers have better means of communication and control, not least management and ownership of most of the public media. In the world of the ancient text, "public media" meant especially the stylized practices of monarchy and temple. "Breaking the silence" is always counter-discourse that tends to arise from the margins of society, a counter to present power arrangements and to dominant modes of social imagination.

To be sure, the breaking of silence is not always positive and constructive, as some silence breakers may also yield destructive voices; we should not romanticize. A case in point of such negative silence breaking is that of the far-right political leader in the Netherlands, Geert Wilders, who lost an election for prime minister in March, 2017. At the instant of his electoral defeat, he declared, "Regardless of the verdict, no one will be able to silence me."[1] Another example is flag burning in the United States. It is such unwelcome speech, but it is protected by the Constitution. Nevertheless, President Trump wants to silence such activists by jail or revocation of citizenship. That, of course, is the risk of allowing for silence breaking, but it is a risk that is indispensable for any human society that is not to drift further toward fascism and the domination of a single voice.

The church has a huge stake in breaking the silence, because the God of the Bible characteristically appears at the margins of established power arrangements, whether theological or socioeconomic and political. The church at its most faithful is allied with artistic expression from the margin that voices alternatives to dominant imagination. Prayer—beyond conventional polite prayer—is an act of breaking the silence. Thus, in the parable of Luke 18:1–8 Jesus tells the disciples to pray like the widow in the narrative: that is, "to pray always and not to lose heart" (v. 1). Intercession, that is, *intrusion into the courts of power on behalf of another*, is central to the church's action in prayer. Gerald Sheppard has, moreover, proposed that the lament and protest prayers of the book of Psalms that critique and assault enemies are designed for being "overheard" by those enemies, who are thereby called to account.

> We may argue that prayer even when spoken in private is a political activity. Prayer requires an economic use of times and places. Prayer seeks to articulate reality, attribute aspects of reality to God, summon God to act, and nurture courage to persevere or pro-

voke change in the conduct of the one who prays. The question is, strictly speaking, not whether prayer is political, but what politics pertain to this or that particular prayer.[2]

The studies offered here are discrete discussions of specific texts. The effect for me however, has been cumulative, and I hope it will be so for the reader. As I have moved from text to text, the company of silence breakers has become more evident to me. Since we now live in a society—and a world—that is fitfully drifting toward fascism, the breaking of silence is altogether urgent. In the institutional life of the church, moreover, the breaking of silence by the testimony of the gospel often means breaking the silence among those who have a determined stake in maintaining the status quo.

It is my hope that these sketches of silence will help us to discern more clearly the way in which our socio-political circumstance, now as always, is an urgent contest between silence and silence breaking. I hope as well that these sketches of silence may constitute a summons to sign on more vigorously with the silence breakers who know, deeply and intimately, that silence kills.

I finish with one more vignette concerning silencing from Lewis Hyde, who reports on a sermon by Charles Chauncy in 1742 titled "A Caveat against Enthusiasm." Chauncy fears the enthusiasts in his context who wanted to sing and dance in worship:

> Chauncy gives his flock instruction on how to recognize the enthusiasts in their midst. That you can't reason with them is the first sign, but, interestingly

enough, all the others have to do with their bodies: "it may be seen in their countenance," "a certain wildness . . . in their general look," "it strangely loosens their tongues," "throws them . . . into quakings and tremblings," they are "really beside themselves, acting . . . by the blind impetus of a wild fancy." It is precisely the feeling that one's body has been entered by some "other" that Chauncy wishes to warn against.[3]

Chauncy saw that such people preferred bodily action rather than talk:

> And the ceremonies of enthusiastic religions tend to include the body, rather than talk. The celebrants dance and sing, they quake and tremble. But no one dances ecstatic dances in the churches of the rich. Nor do they speak in tongues or raise their hands in the gesture of epiphany the way the Christian enthusiasts do. The rich would seem to sense that the more you feel the spirit move in the physical body on Sunday, the harder it will be to trade in cash on Monday. Better to sit in one's pew and listen to talk.[4]

But Chauncy did not even mean "talk." More precisely he meant "listen to a talk," that is, to sit and listen in silence to an authorized voice. Hyde goes on to say that such talk in the church, dominated by "abstraction of symbols" in theology, is deeply linked to the abstract symbol of "cash," thus linking *abstract theology that silences* to the *reduction of life to commoditization and the management of money*. It is, Hyde judges in an appeal to Walt Whitman, reference to the body in its concreteness, which counters such abstractions, that permits domination, monopoly, and exploitation. It has struck me through these several textual studies how silence breaking is evoked by attention to the body in pain. The body knows that silence kills. When the silence is broken, the body may be restored and the body politic may be open to new possibility.

Chapter 1

THE OPPRESSED
BREAK SILENCE

*After a long time the king of
Egypt died. The Israelites groaned under
their slavery, and cried out. Out of the
slavery their cry for help rose up to God.*

—Exod. 2:23

THE CRUCIAL DRAMA OF THE OLD TESTAMENT (AND OF
the entire Bible) concerns the performance of Pharaoh, ancient Israel, and YHWH (see glossary) found
in Exodus 1–15. The story begins with Pharaoh and
ends with YHWH. The one constant in all parts of the
story is Israel, a community that moves from slavery
to emancipated possibility. The Exodus narrative is the
account of how that movement happened . . . and continues to happen.

THE STORY

The lead character at the beginning of the story is Pharaoh, king of Egypt. He might have been an actual
historical character, though his identity is completely

elusive. More importantly, he is a metaphor or stand-in for many historical characters who successively reenact his role. On the one hand, in Egyptian lore he is taken to be a god invested with absolute authority. From that it follows that his regime is all-embracing. Nothing is possible or even imaginable beyond his reach. It also means that his absolute authority and control extend to perpetuity. There is no prospect for anything outside of Pharaoh's absolutism and nothing after it, because there is nothing after perpetuity.

He is ready to exploit cheap labor ruthlessly and without relief. His strictures against his Hebrew labor force are insistent and uncompromising. The only thing he knows to do is to impose greater demands on the slave force and higher production quotas under increasingly difficult conditions (Exod. 5). He exhibits not a hint of awareness that his labor force consists of actual, vulnerable human persons. His incessant pressure on his slave labor force is in the interest of building "store-house cities" designed to store Pharaoh's food monopoly so that he can accumulate a surplus on which all others are eventually dependent (1:11). He had the shrewd capacity to utilize his food monopoly as political leverage. His capacity to do so, however, depended on his ability to store the grain adequately, and for that he needed slave labor. Thus the character of Pharaoh, absolute to perpetuity, was committed to and dependent on a ruthless labor policy to protect and enhance his surplus, which he had at the expense of subsistence peasants.

And then, says the narrative, Pharaoh died (2:23)! His death is a contradiction of his ideology. The ideology asserted "absolute to perpetuity." But then he died. And with his death came dramatic relief from a policy of ruthless exploitation. What had seemed absolute was not! What had been declared to perpetuity was terminated! It turned out that these claims were patently false.

The wonder of the Exodus narrative is that the role of pharaoh continues to be reperformed in many times and many places. "Pharaoh" reappears in the course of history in the guise of coercive economic production. In every new performance, the character of Pharaoh makes claims to be absolute to perpetuity; the character is regularly propelled by fearful greed; the character imposes stringent economic demands on a vulnerable labor force. And characteristically such a performance ends, exposed as false, in death. It is the insistent wisdom of the narrative, always being reperformed and reasserted, that the claim of Pharaoh is a charade. It is, in its moment, every time a powerful charade; but every time it is unsustainable: "[Then] the king of Egypt died" (Exod. 2:23). And when the king of Egypt dies and repeatedly dies in many narrative performances, every time everything becomes unglued, and we learn yet again that there is nothing absolute or perpetual about such claims by the regime.

THE HEBREWS

When Pharaoh dies, room emerges in the story for Israel to make a formidable entry. Up until our verse 2:23 this slave community is often called "Hebrew" (1:15, 16, 19; 2:6, 7, 11, 13). The term *Hebrew* apparently is a sociological one that describes a vulnerable outsider population that was repeatedly "the last hired and the first fired," people who had no legitimate membership in society and were therefore exceedingly vulnerable to the whim of the powerful. In our verse, however, and often in the narrative before our verse, in Exodus 1–2, the company of slaves is not only stylized "Hebrews," but they are called "Israelites." Thus in our verse, "the *Israelites* groaned." Whatever the sociology of the term *Hebrew*, the term *Israelite* is covenantal. Its usage situates this company of slaves in the ongoing drama of covenant with YHWH, the God of promise. This means that for this community, for those in on the sweep of the narrative, the generation present at the death of Pharaoh belonged to the ancient company of Abraham, who, propelled by promise, undertook the risk that they would arrive at the wilderness of *abundance,* at Mount Sinai, pledged to covenantal *obedience*, and eventually at the *land of promise.* All this is not told in the story, but it is assumed in the utterance of the term "Israelite" as in "the Israelites groaned."

What Pharaoh and his ilk could see were the Hebrews (as in Gen. 43:32); the Egyptians could not eat with the Hebrews because it was an "abomination."

The term *Hebrew* . . . describes a vulnerable outsider population that was repeatedly "the last hired and the first fired," people who had no legitimate membership in society and were therefore exceedingly vulnerable to the whim of the powerful.

What appeared in the eyes of Pharaoh to be Hebrews were in truth, as the narrative knows, Israelites marked by covenantal futures and covenantal protection.

Verse 2:23 provides a succinct summary of the story of the Israelites: "They groaned under their slavery." They had ended in helpless, forlorn slave labor in the ruthless predatory system of Pharaoh. The old Pharaoh had been friendly toward the Hebrews and welcomed them. But the new Pharaoh (who remains nameless) "did not know Joseph" (Exod. 1:8), was not bound by old friendship, and so sucked the vulnerable Hebrews into his predatory system. We are not told how that happened. But the narrative of Genesis 47:13–25, speaking not of Hebrews but of other people, suggests that it happened by inevitable and complete dependence on Pharaoh's food monopoly, which made the Hebrews, like many other people, vulnerable to Pharaoh's predation. The move from prosperity under Pharaoh to hopeless slavery was by confiscation of property and their means of production (cattle) and the accumulation of debt from which the Hebrews had no recourse except to submit to Pharaoh's system of economic greed.

Their circumstance of acute vulnerability is described as "brick making" in which the Hebrews are pressed to greater and greater production, even while they are forced to gather their own straw for such production (Exod. 5:7–13). The toil of brick making is rightly termed "hard labor." We know how hard that labor was from parallels in our own time, a process of brick making that likely has not changed from what it was in that ancient day. Pamela Constable described the process of making bricks in contemporary Pakistan:

> The kilns are remote, self-contained worlds, carpeted in thick red dust, where clay-colored figures squat all day in the sun, shaping balls of mud into bricks and setting them out in rows to dry. More than 200,000 migrant laborers work in kilns across Pakistan, earning a few hundred rupees a day. Small children squatted beside their fathers, rolling mud bricks on the quarry floor. Older boys load bricks on the little quarry donkeys, which trudged to the kilns and then trotted back to their own. Soot-streaked men shoveled coal into underground ovens, while chimneys overhead billowed trails of black smoke across the pale dawn sky. The kiln families live in encampments of brick huts beside the quarries, cut off from schools and shops. Most eventually borrow money from the owners and become permanently indebted.[1]

The status of being permanently indebted is by design in that system. Those who owed Pharaoh an unpayable debt were fated to work forever at the demand of Pharaoh. Indeed, when we consider permanent indebtedness of many people in our own predatory economic system, we can see how the drama of Egypt is endlessly reperformed.

The endless reach of the power of debt in contemporary Pakistan eventually dehumanizes and reduces to hopelessness and helplessness:

> Many never earn enough to leave. If they move to a new kiln, their debt moves with them. "It can stay with you for life, like a pair of invisible handcuffs," one worker told me. Kiln work is hot and dangerous, and many workers have old burn marks on their arms

and legs. But there is another horrifying hazard that some willingly risk in their desperation to get out of debt: selling their kidneys in the clandestine organ trade.[2]

For good reason the slaves were reduced to despair and therefore to silence. At most they could quarrel among themselves, but never emit a peep against the regime, for that was too much to dare (Exod. 5:20–21).

In order to grasp the depth of pharaonic enslavement we must reflect on what surely must have happened to those who were hopelessly locked into the debt system of Pharaoh and who knew that there is no exit from pharaonic enslavement. We can imagine that as Hebrews they eventually forfeited their self-consciousness and their historical identification. Many of them must have lived in unrelieved despair and submitted without resilient possibility, finally going through endless motions of brick making without any future at all. Surely they were indeed tired of living, if not scared of dying, and they saw that every day of work left them deeper in debt and without recourse of any kind. Thus, Hebrews without right or prospect is exactly what the predatory economy of Pharaoh required. For good reason the slaves were reduced to despair and therefore to silence. At most they could quarrel among themselves but never emit a peep against the regime, for that was too much to dare (Exod. 5:20–21).

THE SLAVES GROANED

But then he died! The unimaginable happened! The kingpin of predation was gone! He lasted, in the biblical narrative, from Exodus 1:8 to 2:23; it must have seemed an eon to the slaves. When such a brutal predator dies, something of the system of predation dies with him, and new possibilities become imaginable. This moment of Pharaoh's death is a pivotal moment in the biblical story. Indeed, it is a pivotal moment in the history of the world. It is always a pivotal moment in the history of the world when a pharaoh dies. Because what happens is that "the Hebrews" are able to remember and compute the truth that they are "Israelites." And their status as "left-behind" Hebrews is abruptly moved to a re-embrace of their true status as Israelites. Thus in our verse it is not the Hebrews who cried out but the Israelites. It is a moment, in the rhetoric of critical theory, when the victims become conscious, when the slaves become aware that they may be actors in their own history and agents of their own future. Until this moment the Hebrew victims had no consciousness, no sense of being subject, no capacity to be agent. The move to embrace the identity of Israelite is indeed naive, but that naiveté becomes the origin and foundation of thinking critically about history and about one's place in it. Everything depended on that moment of coming to consciousness. The cry and the groan are the beginning of that process that eventuated in a departure from Pharaoh's system.

All of this is accomplished in the terse statement

"The Israelites groaned under their slavery, and cried out" (Exod. 2:23). They announced their presence in history. They brought their suffering and pain to speech, thereby asserting that such suffering as their work in the kilns and such pain as perpetual debt are not normal. In that instant, they entertained, as they had been unable to do before, the possibility that alternative ways of existence are available, ways that were not available as long as Pharaoh was absolute and perpetual, for his ways are the ways of imposed silence.

The cry that breaks the silence is the sound of bodies becoming fully aware of what the predatory system has cost and being fully aware as well that it can be otherwise. Antonio Gramsci asserts that this moment of consciousness by the victim is "the small door through which Messiah may enter."[3] It is a door, an access point that had not been heretofore available (see Rev. 3:20). It is, to be sure, a small door. The erstwhile Hebrew slaves have little chance of such a historical possibility. The vulnerable indebted always have only a little chance, but it is a chance! The messiah who comes is alternative historical possibility that arises from outside the closely administered system of brutalizing silence. Gramsci is thinking critically, not theologically, and certainly not christologically. In biblical context, however, the messiah who comes is exactly a human agent of divine alternative, of whom in the Bible there are many: Moses, Samuel, David, Elijah, Cyrus, and eventually Jesus. But history does not depend alone on the biblical inventory of messiahs. In our own time, that small door of historical alternative has been entered by Gandhi, Mandela, Walesa, Havel, Mao, King,

Gorbachev, and a host of others who have generated historical possibility where none existed.

The cry and groan of the Hebrew slaves was not aimed in any particular direction, not addressed to anyone. It was more generic and amorphous, simply the out-loud disclosure of the unbearable. That declaration of the unbearable is an act of hope. Pharaoh did not care that the slaves suffered (nor does any pharaoh). He assumed that their suffering was simply part of the proper fate of the economically failed. Pharaoh could tolerate their suffering and pain. What he could not tolerate was the voicing of suffering and pain because the voicing sets the juices of alternative in motion. The voicing mobilized the attention and energy of the ones who had no voice. For that reason, Pharaoh is the indispensable, uncompromising silencer who prevents the Hebrews from mobilizing their imaginations and from summoning any would-be ally from beyond.

In this moment of cry and groan the silence is broken, and the silencer is denied. The silence system has failed. Human bodily sounds are made. And with them begins the historical process that ends in "exit" (exodus) and emancipation. All of that is evoked by the wretched breaking of silence. The brutalizing power from above, the royal enforcer of silence, is defeated!

GOD HEARD

Only now, only belatedly, YHWH enters the narrative. The key mode of YHWH in the narrative up to this point is one of *absence*. For two chapters YHWH has been noticeably nonparticipatory. God did indeed "deal well" with the midwives in Exodus 1:20. But that was all surreptitious. Only now does YHWH heed the small door of the cry of the slaves to enter the narrative. Only now, after the cry becomes vigorous, does YHWH become aware of the unbearable situation generated by Pharaoh. That, however, is how the predatory system chooses to work: "Without God everything is possible." Because the slave master is "without God," Pharaoh finds everything possible. Pharaoh finds abuse and exploitation possible. Pharaoh finds accumulation, monopoly, and violence possible because there is no check on Pharaoh's surging autonomy. That is how it is among us. The predatory system has practiced permanent indebtedness without check or restraint and can proceed in pharaonic, uncaring, unnoticing relentlessness.

But then, the silence is broken. The groan is sounded. The cry is uttered. The predatory system is dislocated. The absolutism and perpetuity of Pharaoh are abruptly subverted.

YHWH turned out to be a magnet that drew and continues to draw the cries and groans of the helpless, vulnerable, and indebted who move to YHWH's festival-generating mercy.

At long last God heard! The Hebrew-Israelites who find voice had not addressed YHWH. As Hebrews they had been numbed to amnesia; they did not know the name of any messiah who might enter because they did not know of any possible small door. Unbeknownst to them, their groan and cry created that door.

Their cry, not directed by them, "rose up to God" (Exod. 2:23). Their cry, without any direction from those who cried, knew where to go. The cry understood that its proper destination was the ear of YHWH, for YHWH turned out to be the listener. More than that, YHWH turned out to be a magnet that drew and continues to draw the cries and groans of the helpless, vulnerable, and indebted who move to YHWH's festival-generating mercy. As a result of the arrival of the cry at the attentiveness of YHWH, YHWH in the text is given a full share of responsive verbs:

God heard: The cry does not float off into empty space, but initiates a dialogue that evokes holy power and holy resolve.

God saw: In the later utterance of Israel's lament over destroyed Jerusalem the poet will ask,

> Is it nothing to you, all of you who pass by?
>   Look and see
> if there is any sorrow like my sorrow,
>   which was brought upon me.
> (Lam. 1:12)

And here in our narrative long before, those who groan and cry ask generically about their unbearable burden, "Is it nothing to you?" And here we get an answer. Their cry is not "nothing." This is the God who looks and sees and takes in the sorrow.

God knew: Our translation says, "God took notice" (2:25). But God "knew." God recognized who was speaking. A textual variant, moreover, permits more:

"God knew *them*." God recognized the Hebrew slaves who, only as they cried out, could be seen and known as Israelites. God recognized that these were folk God had already known. These are not strangers to God, but they were not and could not be recognized by God until their self-announcement via groan and cry.

God remembered: Because God heard, saw, and knew (them), God remembered that this moment of engagement was not de novo. It was rooted in the memory of the God of Genesis. Imagine that! The sound of slaves groaning reminded YHWH of the old ancestors Abraham, Isaac, and Jacob, each of whom in failed circumstance had relied on God's inexplicable gift of a future by means of an inexplicable heir.

And now this company without voice in pharaonic circumstance relies on that same gift. This moment of engagement carries the identification of slaves who cry and groan back to the old carriers of God's promise. Jon Levenson early on has protested against the appropriation of this narrative for liberation movements beyond Jews.[4] And surely Jews have first claim on the narrative of emancipation. It requires no illicit imagination, however, to see that the narrative process of identifying those who cry and groan with the promise carriers readily moves into other contexts with other peoples. This God has a wide horizon, and so a much wider population of those who cry and groan have found the text to be compelling for themselves as well. In such an oft-replicated circumstance, the text endlessly reiterates the assurance of YHWH:

"I have observed the misery of my people who are in Egypt; I have heard their cry on account of their taskmasters. Indeed, I know their sufferings, and I have come down to deliver them from the Egyptians, and to bring them out of that land to a good and broad land, a land flowing with milk and honey, to the country of the Canaanites, the Hittites, the Amorites, the Perizzites, the Hivites, and the Jebusites. The cry of the Israelites has now come to me. I have also seen how the Egyptians oppress them." (Exod. 3:7–9)

The bondaged nobodies are now situated in the covenantal story of unconditional promises, the assurance that they will be led to the land of well-being. The Hebrews have become Israelites, carriers of the promises of God. Thus God, in our verse, moves from *absence* to *notice* to *recognition* to *promise*. It is all triggered, however, not by YHWH's faithful will but by the cry that breaks the totalism of Pharaoh. It is the cry, the daring assertion of unbearable suffering, that transposes Hebrews into Israelites. Pharaoh prefers silence that keeps Hebrews hopeless slaves who know nothing except hard labor. But the cry makes Pharaoh's preference null and void. It is no wonder that the initial cry of the slaves ends in the exuberant singing and dancing of Miriam:

"Sing to the LORD, for he has triumphed gloriously; horse and rider he has thrown into the sea."
(Exod. 15:21)

It is the silence-breaking cry that begins the process that turns pain into joy.

QUESTIONS FOR REFLECTION

1. The king of Egypt, like all kings, claimed to have perpetual control over the people. How do "kings" today claim to have control over people?
2. On page 13, the author says, "When we consider permanent indebtedness of many people in our own predatory economic system, we can see how the drama of Egypt is endlessly reperformed." What does he mean?
3. The people cried out, and God heard and acted. Does God require groans in order to act? What can we learn from this story for our time?

Chapter 2

PROPHETS REFUSE TO BE SILENCED

*"Never again prophesy at
Bethel, for it is the king's sanctuary,
and it is a temple of the kingdom."*

—Amos 7:13

THE UNITED KINGDOM OF ISRAEL DID NOT REMAIN UNITED
for long after the reign of King David and son Solomon.
The succession of Solomon's son was rejected by many,
and the monarchy soon split into the northern kingdom of Israel, with its eventual capital city in Samaria,
and the southern kingdom of Judah, with its capital
city of Jerusalem. The royal dynasty of King David,
as portrayed in the biblical text, was a *tax-collecting,
labor-exploiting, surplus-wealth-exhibiting* regime. It lasted
in Jerusalem until the destruction of the city in 587
BCE (see glossary) at the hands of the Babylonians (2
Kgs. 25:8–17). After the northern kingdom of Israel
seceded from the Davidic-Solomonic regime and
formed its own parallel administration, there is no reason to think that the rule of the northern kingdom was

not also a parallel practice of *exploitative tax collection, labor exploitation*, and *surplus wealth exhibition.*

Both regimes, north and south, insofar as they were able, sought to establish an authoritarianism whereby they managed the economy, controlled the political processes, and dominated public imagination. Indeed, in the ancient world the temple (as in Jerusalem in Judah and in Bethel in northern Israel) was the center of media attention, and the several regimes intended to monopolize imagination and to allow nothing outside the scope of their governance. These governing regimes sought to establish a social reality in which alternative imagination or alternative thinking was unlikely to occur.

THE PROPHETIC POETS

In the midst of these autocracies, south and north in ancient Israel, there came to voice from time to time uncredentialled poets without pedigree or authorization who uttered words from outside the regimes. The tradition calls them "prophets." In terms of social reality they appear to have been random utterers of startling poetry that was not contained in the familiar categories or approved reason of the royal leaders and their priests. Their speech was highly stylized, but it nonetheless manages to be in profound touch with actual lived circumstance.

These poets (prophets) interpreted their lived context as if YHWH, the God of the old covenantal traditions, were an actual active agent in historical affairs. Given the assumptions of the old covenantal tradition, they spoke as if the old Ten Commandments were in effect, and as if obeying or not obeying them would determine the future of society, either for good or for evil. Such assumptions deeply contradicted the royal-priestly regimes who assumed that YHWH's unconditional commitment to the chosen people provided a bottomless guarantee of well-being and security. That bottomless guarantee came, so it was assumed, with an unrestrained capacity to conduct an antineighborly economy in the interest of surplus wealth of the urban advantaged at the expense of the economically impotent peasants. This triad of *exploitative labor, unjust taxation*, and *exhibition of surplus wealth* was judged by these poets as both antineighborly and in defiance of the will of the covenantal God. The offensive substance of their poetry was, moreover, matched by offensive imagery as the poets, with immense courage and imagination, utilized savage and daring metaphors in an attempt to pierce the narcotized self-assurance and indifference of the totalitarian regimes.

This triad of *exploitative labor, unjust taxation,* and *exhibition of surplus wealth* was judged by these poets as both antineighborly and in defiance of the will of the covenantal God.

These poets had no credentials or pedigree. They spoke beyond any legitimation from the established regime. In order to have authorized standing ground for their subversive poetry, in various ways they claimed that their poetry came from God. It certainly came from elsewhere beyond the reach or approval of the authorities. Thus the so-called "messenger formula" was regularly utilized: "Thus saith the Lord." That is, the prophets understood that their offensive utterance cast in offensive figure was not their own idea or speech. Rather it was speech given to them by the Holy God of the covenantal tradition. In making that claim, these poets are not unlike our contemporary poets who frequently attest, "The words came to me." Such claims of course could not be tested or verified by conventional establishment criteria. Clearly such utterance beyond the legitimacy of the establishment constituted a threat to royal-priestly claims of ultimacy that were given holy legitimacy through the temples and sanctuaries over which the royal authority presided. No establishment figure wants to tolerate affrontive poetry that exposes the failure of the totalizing system and claims it contradicts God's will.

THE PROPHETIC CHALLENGE

In the historical memory of ancient Israel we have evidence that the royal establishment went to great pains to silence such dangerous, provocative poets. In the poetry of Hosea, the prophets were dismissed as crazy persons:

> The days of punishment have come,
>   the days of recompense have come;
>   Israel cries,
> "The prophet is a fool,
>   the man of the spirit is mad!"
>   (Hos. 9:7)

In a crisis of war when Jerusalem was under siege,

the prophet Jeremiah was labeled a traitor who under-
mined the war effort:

> The officials said to the king, "This man ought to be
> put to death, because he is discouraging the soldiers
> who are left in this city, and all the people, by speak-
> ing such words to them." (Jer. 38:4)

In almost stylized repetition it is reported that the
prophets were killed as enemies of the regime. This was
apparently the case in the northern kingdom during the
intense conflict between the royal practices and policies
of King Ahab and Queen Jezebel on one side and the
faithful resisters who claimed allegiance to YHWH on
the other (1 Kgs. 18:4, 13; 19:1–2, 10, 14; 2 Kgs. 9:7).

Jeremiah himself was on trial for his life and came
very close to a death sentence (26:7–19, 24), being res-
cued only by powerful sympathizers among royal offi-
cials. The story of his trial is followed, moreover, by a
narrative report that another prophet, Uriah, spoke "in
words exactly like those of Jeremiah," and was indeed
sought out and killed by King Jehoiakim (26:20–23).

This tradition of *royal authoritarianism* and of *poetic
(prophetic) interruption* is a rivalry that permeates Israel's tradition. Our attention to this rivalry permits us
to see that in our own time this same contestation is
underway with the royal role performed by a wealthy,
greedy oligarchy and the poetic dissent enacted by a
variety of intrepid advocates who engage a voice from
elsewhere in many forms, from direct political action
to community organizing to comedic mockery to subversive music to relentless artistic exposé. The contest
always remains open and unresolved. This general

contestation between royal totalism and poetic interruption prepares us to consider the dramatic confrontation in our particular text about Amos.

AMOS

Among those unwelcome poetic interrupters came the
prophet Amos. He follows a century after the dramatic
appearance of prophets Elijah and Elisha in northern
Israel (1 Kgs. 17–2 Kgs. 8) and is commonly reckoned
as the first of the great classic prophets in ancient
Israel, that is, the first who left us a literature based on
his utterance. He appeared in northern Israel during
the reign of Jeroboam II, the most successful and pros-
perous of the northern kings (786–746 BCE).

Amos regularly inserted, "Thus says the Lord,"
so that it is clear his utterance comes from elsewhere
beyond the reason or approval of the royal regime in
northern Israel. His words suggest that YHWH, the
God of Israel, is not unlike a marauding lion that is on
the loose in a way that jeopardizes northern Israel. At
the outset the book of Amos (named after the prophet)
introduces his words as the roar of lion YHWH:

> The LORD roars from Zion,
> and utters his voice from Jerusalem.
> (Amos 1:2)

When Amos asserts his own prophetic-poetic
authority, he reports that he has been moved by the
roar of YHWH, the lion God. And when he comes to
speak of the "rescue" of Samaria, the capitol city, from
the hungry rage of the lion (in context the ravaging

Sorting Out Some Names and Dates

The term *Israel* came to be used in a variety of ways over the course of time. *Israelites* is the name given to all the descendants of Jacob, who was also called Israel (Gen. 35:10). Jacob, or Israel, had twelve sons, the ancestors of the twelve tribes of Israel. One of these sons was Judah. Things became confusing hundreds of years later when, two generations after King David's reign, the kingdom of Israel split into two nations. The northern kingdom continued to call itself Israel, with capital Samaria, and the southern kingdom took the name of its largest tribe, Judah, with capital Jerusalem.

But after the northern kingdom was destroyed by Assyria in the eighth century BCE, *Israel* once again became available as a name for all the descendants of Jacob, including the Judeans. At this point the names became somewhat interchangeable. Though the political name of the nation that was left remained *Judah* (and later *Judea*), and though the terms *Judaism, Jew,* and *Jewish* derive from this name, *Israel* continued to be used side by side with these terms.

The other three names are easier to distinguish. *Jerusalem* is the city in Judah that King David adopted as his capital. *Zion* is another name for Jerusalem. *Canaan* identifies the physical land that the Israelites occupied, because it was originally inhabited by Canaanites.

Key Dates and Prophets

1,000 BCE	King David reigns.
922 BCE	Israel divides into north (Israel) and south (Judah, which includes Jerusalem) after Solomon dies.
Key Northern Prophets	Elijah, Elisha, Amos, Hosea
786–746 BCE	Amos prophesies in the north during the reign of Jeroboam II.
722 BCE	The Assyrians destroy and annex the north.
Key Southern Prophets	Isaiah, Micah, Habakkuk, Zephaniah, Jeremiah, Ezekiel
587 BCE	The Babylonians destroy the south and exile many leaders.
587–538 BCE	The exile in Babylon (see glossary).

Assyrian army), he describes the leftovers from a hungry lion as the wee remnant of northern Israel to be left behind:

> Thus says the LORD: As the shepherd rescues from the mouth of the lion two legs, or a piece of an ear, so shall the people of Israel who live in Samaria be rescued, with the corner of a couch and part of a bed. (Amos 3:12)

The verb "rescue" is precisely "snatch," that is, snatched out of the mouth of a lion at the last instant. Amos sees that the political-economic life of northern Israel is in radical contradiction to the will of YHWH, and therefore the royal state can have no viable future. The geopolitical expression of that threat from YHWH is in the form of the expansive policies of Assyria (present-day Iraq) that Israel could not resist.

The narrative report of Amos 7:10–17 is in response to this stance, seen in verse 9, in which Amos speaks of YHWH's harsh judgment against the "house" (that is, dynasty) of King Jeroboam:

> "The high places of Isaac shall be made desolate,
>   and the sanctuaries of Israel shall be laid waste,
>   and I will rise against the house of Jeroboam with
>   the sword."

In response to this oracle, Amaziah, the priest who presided over the important temple at Bethel, sent word to King Jeroboam about the threat posed by the poetry of Amos (7:10–11). Two matters interest us in this opening statement by Amaziah. First, the priest misquotes the poet. Amos had said that "the house of Jeroboam" would suffer, but he never cited the king per se. In his misquote the priest makes the poetry of Amos more personal in its attack, as if it were a direct assault on the king himself, which it is not. Second, the priest invokes the ominous word "conspire," a term that intends to suggest a deliberate strategy for the overthrow of the dynasty. Thus when Amos speaks the truth of the covenantal tradition, it sounds like treason to the priest.

The priest does not await a response from the king. He knows what to do. He acts on what he knows the king would have said, namely, "You must silence the poet." The poet must be silenced because his dangerous utterance would serve in popular opinion to delegitimate a king who violates the will of the covenant God. Thus the priest turns promptly from addressing the king (who never appears in the narrative) to addressing the prophet (v. 12). He issues an order of banishment of Amos not only from the temple over which the priest presides but also from the land of northern Israel over which the king presides. Amos had come from Judah in the south, and now the priest dispatches him back there. The phrase "earn your bread there" suggests that the prophet was at his work for money, thus trivializing and dismissing his urgent word. What interests us is the reason the priest offers for the expulsion of the poet: "'Never again prophesy at Bethel, for it is the king's sanctuary, and it is a temple of the kingdom'" (v. 13).

The poet must be silenced because his dangerous utterance would serve in popular opinion to delegitimate a king who violates the will of the covenant God.

The temple belongs to and serves the king and royal interests, as all ancient temples have done. In that temple, all that could be said—in liturgy, instruction, and proclamation—must be in line with the interests of the royal establishment. No other words are allowed, no word of judgment or critique or negation, a prohibition that comes to mean "no truth telling." And of course many churches in our own time are simply chapels for the establishment, in which those who speak in church are expected to support establishment claims and so to "show the flag." No other voice is allowed in the required collusion of liturgy and established interests.

Amos makes two rejoinders to his expulsion. First, he dissents from the priest's accusation that he does his poetic work "for bread." He is a "tent-maker" poet, not a professional one. This is not his "job." His job, as a tent-maker, is to be a shepherd, a quite menial assignment. What he does in truthful utterance to which the priest objects is not a job from which he can be fired. He is under assignment from the Lord who has confronted him directly and dispatched him to such utterance. His statement is an insistence that the priest, or the king for whom the priest speaks, has no authority to banish him. The prophet is not subject to such royal silencing.

In the wake of that reassertion of authority from elsewhere, Amos then utters a poem that makes clear his refusal to be silenced by priestly dictate. In 7:16 Amos reiterates the formula of banishment from the priest. Only he revises the words of the priest; he is also capable of misquoting! Now it is not "the house of Jeroboam" but the "house of Isaac" as the prophet reaches back more deeply into the tradition. Amos, for inexplicable reasons, has already linked "the high places of Isaac" with the "house of Jeroboam" in 7:9 and now reiterates that enigmatic connection.

But what we notice is that verse 17 is introduced by the formidable and prophetic "Therefore." That is, as a result of this priestly attempt at banishment (v. 16), Amos repeats a judgment against the royal apparatus and then intensifies his more general indictment, making it immediately personal. Now the judgment is pronounced against the priest. God's sure dismantling judgment is certain in this voicing:

> **Your wife** will have become a vulnerable prostitute, for the coming army of Assyria will, like every invading army, abuse highly placed women.
> **Your sons and daughters** will die in the military assault.
> **Your land**, the land of Northern Israel, will be reassigned and redeployed among the military winners (or among the locals who had colluded with the coming army).
> **You** will die elsewhere, deported out of the land of Israel, to a land not governed by God.
>
> (aut. trans.)

And then, after judgments against Amaziah's wife, sons and daughters, and land, Amos's ultimate judgment is the priest's exilic deportation to a strange land. Amos's anticipation of exile in 7:17 is quite personal toward Amaziah, but the priest is surely the point person for the privileged elite in Samaria. They will all go! It is reported in 2 Kings 14:29 that Jeroboam "slept with his ancestors," that is, died in his own land; he was not deported. But the king per se was never the target of the poet. The target was the narcotized population of the elite who lived off economic surplus and who never noticed the sufferings that their policies and practices imposed on the vulnerable who sustained them by their labor.

The evidence of the Amos tradition, as given to us in the book that bears his name, is that the formula of silencing pronounced by the priest did not work. Amos

was not and could not be silenced. Thus, Amos continues to speak "unhindered" and has the last word with
Amaziah. The priest does not speak again and appears
to have been silenced by Amos's poetic insistence.
Unlike the priest, this uncredentialed poet continues
to speak, unsilenced. In his tradition, moreover, he
continues to speak an unwelcome word amid his self-
deceived society that featured bad labor policy, unfair
taxation, and shameless exhibits of surplus wealth. His
refusal of royal-priestly silence evoked a vision of an
"end," a prospect that was surely illicit in the royal-
priestly temple.

QUESTIONS FOR REFLECTION

1. Why does the author call prophets "poets"?
2. Prophets claim to speak words from God that
   challenge establishment priests and leaders.
   Name someone you believe is a prophet in our
   time and how that person challenges the establishment with words from God.
3. The establishment tries to silence prophets and
   discredit them. Why must they silence prophets,
   and what are ways that they do this?
4. The author says that the temple "belongs to and
   serves the king and royal interests, as all ancient
   temples have done." Where do you see instances
   of this today?
5. What is the purpose of prophets breaking silence?

Chapter 3

SILENCE KILLS

While I kept silence, my body wasted away
through my groaning all day long. . . .

Then I acknowledged my sin to you,
and I did not hide my iniquity;
I said, "I will confess my transgressions to the LORD,"
and you forgave the guilt of my sin.

—Ps. 32:3, 5

AS LONG AGO AS THE SIXTH CENTURY CE, THE CHURCH
had identified seven "penitential psalms." They are
Psalms 6, 32, 38, 51, 102, 130, and 143. These psalms
give voice to the genuine honesty of serious prayer in
which the speaker acknowledges need for God, reliance on God, and confidence in God's goodness. These
seven psalms were crucial for Martin Luther's insight
into the grace-filled generosity of God. Luther termed
these psalms "Pauline psalms" because he found in
them the grace of God that Paul so powerfully exposited
in his letters to the Romans and the Galatians. Among
these seven psalms our focus here is on Psalm 32, a
poem-prayer that moves from *silence* concerning guilt
and alienation to *speech* and thus to gladness and joy.

Our study will focus on the assertion of verse 3 concerning the high cost of silence and on verse 5 about the emancipatory, transformative possibility made possible by speech. Thus far in our work our studies have considered the coercive silence imposed by external authority, such as Pharaoh in Egypt and the priest Amaziah at Bethel. Now in Psalm 32 we face silence that was not externally coerced but was rather a personal decision of repression.

I KEPT SILENT

In verse 3 the psalmist declares, "I kept silent." The speaker does not tell us why. We soon learn, however, that the silence chosen by the speaker is a cover for an acute awareness of sin and iniquity that has alienated the speaker from God and, as a result, from the speaker's own life. We are given no explanation for silence, but we know from our own experience about this strategy for coping with guilt. On the one hand, such chosen silence may be due to social *shame*, peer pressure, and social expectation. It is too embarrassing to name and own one's deep failings; as long as they are unvoiced, we may be allowed to pretend they do not exist. Or on the other hand, such chosen silence may be because of *fear* of rejection and punishment, perhaps from those human persons whom we have disappointed or betrayed, or finally because of one's fear of the anger of God, whose exacting expectation many of us have been taught. Or of course such chosen silence may be the result of *moral insensibility* and an inability even to notice or to reckon with the deep alienation that one's life has come to embody. And if the alienation is unnoticed, then it surely will remain unacknowledged and unvoiced.

It is too embarrassing to name and own one's deep failings; as long as they are unvoiced, we may be allowed to pretend it is not so.

The psalmist does not tell us why silence has been chosen. Rather the psalmist details the cost of such silence. Put most succinctly, what we know and what the psalmist knows is that silence kills. But here the psalmist is dying a little at a time, because the body of the speaker knows the truth. We may deceive our neighbors; we may even fool ourselves about guilt and alienation. But we cannot fool our bodies. Our bodies suffer in ways we eventually notice when they must become the carriers of such denial and deception. Thus the psalmist reports on the result of silence:

My strength was dried up as by the heat of summer.
(v. 4b)

Verse 3 offers a conundrum because after the verb of silence we get a "groan." Such a sound, however, is not an intentional utterance; it is the sound of a body in anguish. For when the psalmist will not speak, the body will find ways to make its own sound of protest and pain.

That trouble that followed chosen silence is evoked "by [God's] hand." Thus in this simple, straightforward

manner the psalmist does not bother with psychoso-
matic analysis but simply and directly credits the bodily
affliction to the power of YHWH. Insofar as this is
God's doing (which the psalmist does not doubt), the
bodily trouble is not evoked by guilt but by silence. Thus
silence brings bodily trouble that comes from God. The
result, moreover, is that the life of the speaker shriv-
els up as a heat wave that wilts the vitality of grass or
flower.

I WILL CONFESS; I WILL NOT COVER UP

The speech of the psalmist makes an abrupt pivot in
verse 5. There is no grammatical marker in the original
Hebrew, not even "then" as we have it in our English
translations. It is as though the speaker can no longer maintain the silence. The pain of bodily affliction
is too acute. In this dramatic moment the one who
had chosen the silence of denial must, perforce, now
choose speech that breaks silence. The word order of
the Hebrew is worth notice as it is not reflected in our
usual translations. In two quick parallel statements the
speaker moves out of silence:

> My sin I have made known;
> My iniquity I do not cover up.
> (Ps. 32:5; au. trans.)

In this perfect parallelism, the objects of the verbs
(*sin, iniquity*) come first as the accent point. They are
followed by first-person resolve that contradicts the
preceding silence. We do not know why the silence is
broken, only that it is. Likely it is broken because the

speaker came to see that the silence was worse than the guilt or alienation. We are given no hint of what the sin was, because the sin itself is of little interest to the speaker or to God. What counts is that the speaker "made known" and did not "cover up," a resolve enforced by yet a third verb, "will confess" (v. 5), now with a third parallel object, his "transgressions." The verb "confess" means to tell the narrative, thus to narrate the affront fully in its context. There is no interest in the nature of the sin, because these verses are preoccupied with the enormous benefit of breaking silence and moving to honest speech before God.

> Here there is described a very different method of acknowledging sin; namely, when the sinner willingly betakes himself to God, building his hope of salvation not on stubbornness or hypocrisy, but on supplication for pardon. This voluntary confession is always conjoined with faith; for otherwise the sinner will continually seek lurking-places where he may hide himself from God.[1]

YOU FORGAVE

The transition is completed in the terse final line of verse 5 that follows without pause, marker, or condition nor delay or reprimand. In addition to the pronoun "you" that attaches to the verb "forgive" ("lift"), the line utilizes the independent pronoun "you" for additional emphasis, so that we might translate, "And *you, you* forgave." The speaker is in no doubt about who it is who responds to the confession. It is the "you" of God already signaled by "I acknowledged my sin to *you*." The silent psalmist has been in a bubble of isolation, imagining for a time—perhaps a long time—that he could suck it up and gut out the guilt. The desperate decision to speak out, however, breaks the isolation that has become unmanageable and unbearable. The speaker reconnects to the "Thou" who can do the forgiveness that the speaker could not do for self. In this moment of acknowledgment the speaker names the name, YHWH. It is to YHWH that his truth must be spoken. The final line indicates that God is ready, willing, and able to forgive, surely only waiting for honest speech that breaks the denial of silence. God would not, or could not, make such a move as long as the denial persisted.

Thus in these three verses we have three dramatic moves. First, a resolve of silence that turns out to be acutely disabling; second, a bold, abrupt breaking of the silence in candor; and third, a prompt generous response from YHWH who restores to life. In the final line of verse 5 attention is turned from "I" to "You," from guilt and alienation to risky restoration and glad rehabilitation.

GOD, THE FAITHFUL LISTENER

This same transformative possibility is articulated precisely in 1 John 1:8–10, which we may take as an early exposition of our psalm:

> If we say we have no sin, we deceive ourselves, and the truth is not in us. If we confess our sins, he who is faithful and just will forgive us our sins and cleanse us from all unrighteousness. If we say that we have not sinned, we make him a liar, and his word is not in us.

The two options are stated with parallel if-clauses: "If we . . . deceive. . . . If we confess." It is only the second option that evokes the one who is "faithful and just" and who readily forgives.

The key insight is that honest *talk* transforms and emancipates when it is received in faithful seriousness.

Thus the succinct report of transformation in Psalm 32:3–5, echoed in 1 John 1:8–10, sums up what we in our modern era have long been learning from Freud that has eventuated in the pastoral care movement.[2] Freud surely drew on his Jewish legacy, even as he refused Jewish identity, and gave contemporary articulation to the very old wisdom of the Israelite covenantal tradition. The key insight is that honest *talk* transforms and emancipates when it is received in faithful seriousness. Freud was permitted to see that the faithful seriousness that in the Psalter pertains to YHWH can be replicated by human agents; thus the God-claim of the Psalms has among us morphed in contemporary practice into the role of pastors, pastoral counselors, and a variety of therapists. The key insight is a *theological* one, that is, it concerns the astonishing readiness of the God of covenant. In contemporary parlance, that theological reality has been transposed into a *psychological transaction*, but the theological root continues to be important because, as Martin Buber understood, the ultimate Thou who is beyond human management is wrapped in impenetrable mystery.

This elemental, transformative capacity through honest speech that refuses silence is peculiarly affirmed by the Psalter. The testimony of the Psalms is so urgent because the seduction of current consumerism is to imagine that in the place of such an unmanageable Thou we may count on *commodity*, or on *instrumental reason* that screens out human issues and human possibility, or on *technological fixes* that leave the future in our own hands. But of course the psalmist tells otherwise, and we know better. Humanness depends on being faithfully heard. And being faithfully heard depends on risky speech of self-disclosure uttered in freedom before a faithful listener. When our psalmist dared to speak, he came to know the name of that faithful listener.

TESTIMONY, PEDAGOGY, DOXOLOGY

It is impossible to overstate the dramatic turn that is accomplished by the move from repressed denial in silence to the release of honest speech faithfully received. Any of us who have been able to make that move can attest to the unmistakable wonder of such a turn. I suggest three responses to the turn that are evident in the psalm.

First there is *testimony* that is a second-level reflection on the wonder of the transition from silence to speech (vv. 1–2). It is wondrous to be forgiven. It makes viable life possible. The double line in verse 2, again introduced by "Happy," depends on two negatives and actually names YHWH, whose name we have found in verse 5. Here well-being is grounded in the reality that YHWH acknowledges or attributes (*hsv*) no guilt to one;

the second line, also as a negative, speaks of YHWH's life-giving *ruah* that has no deceit and will not engage with those who are deceitful. These two verses make a general claim from what has been lived and experienced in the actual transition of verses 3–5.Well-being is on offer for those who relate to YHWH in ways unimpeded by unspoken sin, transgression, iniquity, or deceit. Any and all of these negatives preclude happiness.

Second, verses 8–10 offer *pedagogical advice*. The speaker is eager to share what the speaker has learned and thus becomes a teacher to others who may follow the speaker's own experience in the move from silence to speech. The speaker is fully confident of knowing something important, and so "will gladly instruct" (give prudential advice), that is "practical theology": "I will teach"; "I will counsel." The lesson to be imparted is "the way," the path of candor.

The instruction becomes more vigorous (i.e., tough love) in verse 8 with a negative warning about what to avoid. The negative imperative is "Don't be stupid." Don't be stubborn like a horse that cannot be guided. Don't be a dumb-ass! The psalmist can remember being stupid, not ready to be honest. Or said differently, "Do not do what I did." Don't close down in silence and think you can manage all alone. "What I learned the hard way you can now know without all the hardship and affliction that I faced."

Third, the movement of the psalm is away from a managed self to a yielding self, given over to God in confident trust and eventually in *doxology* (praise). The ones prepared for active fidelity are in contrast to the tormented who go it alone in toxic autonomy.

In the end, those who have broken the silence and come face-to-face with the generous, faithful God live unencumbered lives. They are the ones who are "glad," who "rejoice," and who "shout for joy" (v. 11). Such self-abandoning exuberance is quite in contrast to the "dried up" selves in verse 4 who have never run the risk of honesty. In our previous studies we have seen the cost of social suppression. Now in a parallel fashion we see the cost of personal repression. The alternative to such repression and denial is self-exposure before God that culminates in *testimony, pedagogy*, and *doxology*, all actions that are thick with dialogical engagement. It takes little imagination to recognize that the powerful ideology of individualism that governs so much of our society is pernicious. That awareness was fully operative in ancient Israel (or anywhere else) where the alternative doxological wonder of YHWH was embraced seriously.

QUESTIONS FOR REFLECTION

1. How is the need to break oppressive silence in this chapter similar to or different from that of previous chapters?
2. Describe an experience you have had where keeping silent has hurt you. If you spoke up, how did your feelings change as a result? Was it helpful?
3. The author speaks of YHWH as an alternative to the powerful ideology of individualism. How does breaking silence before God help one join YHWH's movement?

Chapter 4

JESUS RUDELY
INTERRUPTED

*But she answered him, "Sir, even the
dogs under the table eat the children's crumbs."*

—Mark 7:28

ACCORDING TO THE GOSPEL OF MARK, JESUS' MINISTRY
was conducted in Galilee, the central hill country north
of Jerusalem (see 1:9, 14, 16, 28, 39). That territory
was inhabited by peasants and subsistence farmers who
gladly heard his words. Although occupied by the mili-
tary of the Roman Empire, it was otherwise a homoge-
nous population of Jews. As a child of Nazareth, Jesus
conducted his ministry of stunning transformation by
word and action among his own kind of people.

THE BACKGROUND

Among the remarkable acts of his ministry remembered by Mark, in the chapter just before our text, Jesus
reperforms Moses' wonder of bread in the wilderness

(6:30–44; see Exod. 16:13–21). Mark reports that Jesus found a hungry crowd "in a deserted place." He had compassion for them. In response to their hunger and out of his compassion, he performed a sequence of acts that have become the defining sacramental mantra of the church: He took; he blessed; he broke; and he gave (v. 41). The result of his lordly act is that five thousand people were fed with twelve baskets of surplus bread, enough for all twelve tribes of Israel. He is a generous giver of ample bread!

In chapter 7, our chapter, he joins issue with Pharisees and scribes who had come from Jerusalem (Mark 7:1–23). In the Gospel narrative "Jerusalem" is the antithesis of "Galilee," so that we may expect conflict between the Jerusalem authorities and this man from Galilee (see Mark 11:27). The authorities from Jerusalem were intruders in the peasant environment of Galilee and had no doubt come to check out Jesus, of whom they had heard reports. While he disputes with them about purity, the text shows that he, not unlike them, had a significant concern about purity, even if he differed greatly from them in his characterization of proper purity.

THE GENTILE WOMAN

When we come to our narrative text (7:24–30), we find Jesus safely ensconced in a house where he hoped to avoid public attention. Presumably he had been welcomed into that house and was enjoying the hospitality of his host. That scenario of hospitality was, however, sharply and rudely interrupted. A Gentile woman barged into the house. In Mark she is identified as a woman of Syro-Phoenician origin, that is, from the territory to the north of Israel. In the story as told by Matthew, she is identified as a Canaanite woman (Matt. 15:22). Her identity is not clear in the memory of the Gospel writers; all that is clear is that she was a non-Jew who had pushed into a Jewish environment where she did not belong and where she was not welcome. She was an ethnic "other"; beyond that, she was a woman crowding into "manly space" in patriarchal society. On all counts her arrival was disruptive and disturbing. She had, however, come on urgent business. She knew of Jesus' reputation as a healer; her daughter was demon occupied. She knew that Jesus had mastered demons (see Mark 1:34). And like any other passionate parent, she was quite willing, without hesitation, to violate protocols in order to get help and relief for her beloved daughter.

When Jesus brushed away her request, she did not leave. Instead she insisted in crossing boundaries. She is desperate; she bowed down at his feet in deference, and she begged him. She comes with no pride, no sense of entitlement. Jesus is for her a court of last resort. But she does not care about proper protocol; she cares only for her daughter, who is in great need.

OPPRESSIVE SILENCE IS BROKEN

In Mark's narrative Jesus speaks first. In his usual evasive, enigmatic style, Jesus spoke using an image: "'Let the children be fed first, for it is not fair to take the children's food and throw it to the dogs'" (7:27). It is their food! Jesus contrasts "children" and "dogs." Children come first; they should get what is on offer. The image is not explained, but it is understood by all parties. The "children" are the entitled Jews of his own population in Galilee. They should come first. He comments on "food." It is as though he reverts back to his bread wonder (wonder bread!) in chapter 6. Perhaps he is remembering that there were twelve baskets of bread left over, enough for all twelve tribes of Israel, but no more than enough for all Israel.

Now for the first time the woman speaks. She must have spoken earlier when she "begged" Jesus and stated her urgent request to him. That petition, however, is not quoted or reported by Mark. Now in verse 27, she speaks for the first time. She breaks the silence. It must have been a very long silence, for she was a woman in "manly space" as well as an outsider (Syro-Phoenician or Canaanite) in Jewish space. As long as she kept silent, there would be no interruption by an outsider. As long as she kept silent, there would be no intrusion by a woman. We may imagine, moreover, that she had kept silent a very long time, like all outsiders among Jews, like all women among men. All parties in the house where she was present expected the silence to last a long while longer. But now the silence is broken. It is broken in desperate need. She dared to speak on behalf of her possessed daughter.

Mark introduces the desperate mother's speech with an antagonistic conjunction: "But." "But she said," as Elisabeth Schüssler Fiorenza has made famous in her perceptive, daring exposition.[1] She contradicts Jesus. She exposes his insider mentality. She does not do so, moreover, by a comment about ethnic outsiders or about women. Rather she goes along with his imagery about food, children, and dogs: about who should get food first and who should not get food at all. She

---

She even accepted the premise of Jesus that the children should get food first. She does not dispute that point. She only insists that "crumbs," the leftovers (perhaps twelve baskets of leftovers) should be passed along to the "dogs."

---

understands, as does Jesus, that their talk is not in fact about food. In this conversation food functions to illustrate other matters, namely, the power of transformative emancipation. It is a dispute about who possesses such emancipatory power and who should benefit from such power. Her capacity and willingness to go along with the imagery suggests that she is cast not only as a desperate mother but also as a skilled, artistic voice. We did not know when she broke the silence that she would participate in and advance such artistry. We had not expected this other surprise in her utterance. She even accepted the premise of Jesus that the children should get food first. She does not dispute that point. She only insists that "crumbs," the leftovers (perhaps twelve baskets of leftovers) should be passed along to the "dogs."

So now the symbolic allusion is clear. The "children" are the Jews, as we have known all along, the entitled ones cast as chosen, who come first and have priority. The *"dogs,"* as we have known all along, are the "other," the outsider, the Gentile, the Syro-Phoenician woman and her daughter or, as Matthew has it, the Canaanites, so long contested and despised by Israelites. And the "food" is the transformative capacity of God's good power that has been peculiarly entrusted to the life and body of Jesus. She understood the code and willingly claims it for her own advocacy.

When the imagery is decoded, the argument of this outsider woman who dares to speak is that God's transformative capacity for goodness should not and cannot be monopolized by Jews, because it will spill over beyond that. The disputatious conjunction "But," whereby she contradicts Jesus, suggests that Jesus' own sense of his identity and ministry was only to Jews. He was from Galilee. He apparently understood himself, in Markan horizon, in the limited provincial categories of Jewish Galilee, and that was the proper scope of his ministry. There had thus far been no challenge to that scope. There was enough to do in Galilee among Jewish peasants. There were enough needy peasants who had been "left behind" who welcomed his eman-cipatory presence. His own people had received him gladly, and that was surely enough, even if the Jerusalem authorities objected. It had been a tacit assumption that this was his assignment.

JESUS IS CHALLENGED

And now she speaks! She violates the tacit assumption. She intrudes, interrupts, contradicts, and tells other-wise. She calls into question his own sense of his own life. She reeducates him. Such reeducation can never come from those who are comfortable with accepted practices and assumptions. Reeducation comes from voices that dissent from the unexamined comfort zone, from those who abrasively shock our comfort zones with voices from outside that violate the consensus that has been silently accepted. Jesus is a child of his place and time. We are led in this text to assume that Jesus, like his neighbors in context, accepted the consensus that God's "food" was for Jews! She broke that tacit consensus by her insistence, which she managed to articulate within the bounds of his chosen metaphor.

Reeducation comes from voices that dissent from the unexamined comfort zone, from those who abrasively shock our comfort zones with voices from outside that violate the consensus that has been silently accepted.

WHAT WOULD JESUS DO?

Jesus has been addressed beyond silence, and now he must answer. Would he dispute with her? Would he defend male privilege? Would he argue for Jewish chosenness? Would he stubbornly insist that he had it right the first time: He has no ministry to the "dogs"?

No; he does none of that. He makes a different response. He commends the bold woman. His terse comment in verse 29 ends the encounter, but he ends it on her terms. Because she broke the silence in a daring, insistent way that reeducated him, her daughter is set free, just as she had asked. Her emancipation is not a reward for her chutzpah. It is rather that her passion and courage have pushed Jesus' ministry and his healing capacity out beyond the conventional consensus of Galilee. Her speech into that taken-for-granted silence has opened the world anew, not only for her daughter but for many others to follow.

We may expect, after the encounter, that Jesus would enact his ministry in new directions. And indeed he does! In the very next verse, Mark tells us that Jesus moved into the "region of the Decapolis," that is, the zone of the ten Greek cities (7:31). He moved promptly into the zone to which her world-opening speech had summoned him. And there, in Greek territory among Gentiles, he healed a man who was deaf and mute, unable to speak (7:37). He was summoned by this woman's daring speech to move to a venue where he had not thought to go. We may, moreover, imagine that when the restored man could speak, he spoke Greek, the language of the Gentiles.

Beyond that, in Mark 8:1–10, Jesus performs yet another feeding miracle. He has been instructed by the woman about the distribution of food. This time we get the familiar four-fold sacramental mantra in slightly varied form but to the same effect: He took; he gave thanks; he broke; he gave (8:6). Here he begins with "seven loaves" (8:3), and he finishes with seven baskets of bread (8:8). The double use of "seven" is an allusion to the "seven nations" that ancient Israel had displaced in the old Israelite tradition (see Deut. 7:1; Acts 13:19). These nations had been forcibly displaced, and their religious icons had been violently destroyed. But now

Jesus sets them alongside his own people in Galilee as those who are able to share with Jews the "food" of the new regime of God. The woman's speech has set in motion a wholly different history. And we have arrived at a narrative symmetry of *twelve baskets of bread for the twelve tribes of Israel* and *seven baskets of bread for the seven nations* of the tradition. Both the tribes of Israel and the nations of the world are encompassed in the sacramental mantra; both are to receive the transformative power that gives new life. We may read the new interface of "children/dogs" in one of two ways. Either the Gentiles as "dogs" are now reckoned alongside the real children of privilege and chosenness, or the dogs have ceased to be dogs and have become children, that is, among the chosen. Now it is no longer "bread for the chosen people." Now it is "bread for the world." Jesus turned out to be an apt student, and the outsider woman was an effective teacher and witness. He was a quick learner and put his new learning to immediate and effective use.

SILENCE PROTECTS PRIVILEGE

We may pause to consider what this woman has done. By her desperate behavior and her cunning reasoning she has cracked open the old order of male purity and tribal privilege. No wonder she was an unwelcome intruder. She set in motion a new trajectory of transformative possibility that was not on the horizon of the narrative until she broke the silence. It is her contradiction in 7:28 that moves Mark's narrative from the

Jewish feeding wonder of 6:30–44 to the Gentile feed-ing wonder of 8:1–10.

Beyond that, she gave new possibilities for self-understanding to the earliest church:

> The story of the Syro-Phoenician makes women's contribution to one of the most crucial traditions in early Christian beginnings historically available. Through such an analysis, the Syro-Phoenician can become visible again as one of the apostolic fore-mothers of Gentile Christians. By moving her into the center of the debate about the mission to the Gen-tiles, the historical centrality of Paul in this debate becomes relativized.[2]

In the book of Acts it is conventional to give Paul primary credit for the mission to the Gentiles. Theo-logian Elisabeth Schüssler Fiorenza shows that this conventional claim is deconstructed by this story, for it suggests an earlier and different origin by which the earliest church broke out of tribal-ethnic identity. And since our narrative in Mark 7:24–30 follows the debate about purity (Mark 7:1–23), it is no stretch at all to link this narrative and its woman protagonist to the "trance" of Peter in Acts 10 where the issue of purity is exposed. In that narrative Peter, via a trance, is instructed by God to unlearn his earlier commitment to Israel's purity codes. By these codes Peter, like every serious Jew of his time, had convincing clarity about what was ritually clean and acceptable and what was ritually unclean, unacceptable, and dangerous. In this inexplicable confrontation, Peter is summoned by a heavenly voice that declares to him,

"What God has made clean, you must not call pro-
fane." This happened three times, and the thing was
suddenly taken up to heaven. (Acts 10:15–16)

Peter abruptly, like Jesus in our narrative, has a rapid,
dramatic unlearning of old reliable rules of purity. In
the narrative that follows, Peter is led to acknowledge,
"I truly understand that God shows no partiality, but in
every nation, anyone who fears him and does what is
right is acceptable to him" (Acts 10:34–35). Thus, Jesus
experienced, in our narrative, his own people deprivi-
leged; similarly, Peter faced and embraced new possibilities that contradicted the old edicts that defined ritual
purity and social power. In Peter's case that disclosure
set in motion the expansive missional trajectory of the
church, even before Paul was on the scene.

Silence and tacit consensus always, without fail,
protect privilege. That is why the privileged are characteristically silencers. Conversely, contesting speech
characteristically exposes the ideological force of the
silence and privilege and invites us to a fresh take on
the reality of God's world. It is clear, is it not, that the
intrusive, interruptive speech of this unwelcome outsider woman is now being reiterated and replicated in
many different venues in our world, every time to call
into question silently assumed and assured entitlements
and privileges. Before our very eyes we are watching
the undoing of

Silence and tacit consensus always, without
fail, protect privilege. That is why the
privileged are characteristically silencers.

White privilege by multicultural possibilities

Western privilege by the assertion of other cultural realities

Male privilege by insistent feminine voices

Heterosexual privilege by the legitimacy of LGBT voices and presence

American exceptionalism by the rise of other political economies

Entitled Christendom by the emergence of generous ecumenism

It is all as unsettling for many now as it must have been for Jesus, and then for Peter, and for the earliest church. The good news is that with such undoing and violation of the old certitudes of silence come a demon-emancipated daughter, a deaf-mute man restored to full communication, and bread for the world, all breaks with the old consensus. Good things happen when the silence is broken. Our tradition in faith is a long history of inconvenient interruptions.

QUESTIONS FOR REFLECTION

1. Had you read the story of the Syro-Phoenician woman before? How did you understand it then as compared to now?
2. How does the woman challenge Jesus and change his ministry?
3. The author lists a few groups who are speaking out and challenging privilege today. What do you think of this list? Are there other groups you can think of that challenge privilege?

Chapter 5

CASTING OUT SILENCE

*"He has a spirit that makes him unable
to speak; and whenever it seizes him, it dashes
him down; and he foams and grinds his teeth
and becomes rigid; and I asked your disciples
to cast it out, but they could not do so."*

—Mark 9:17–18

THE STORY OF AN EXORCISM IN MARK 9:14–29 STAGES A contest between *the power to silence* and *the power to speak.* The contest is conducted in and through the body of the boy, son of a distraught father. The boy has been silenced. His body is occupied territory, occupied by the power of silence.

THE CAST

This complex narrative features an extended cast of characters. In addition to the boy, the venue of the contest, and his father who desperately seeks help, there are *the crowd, the scribes,* and *the disciples.*

The crowd merits only mention in the narrative. They are only witnesses. We are told that the crowd ran to Jesus and was "overcome with awe" (v. 15). The purpose of the crowd is to call attention to the wonder of Jesus, a wonder that will only be enhanced by the outcome of this narrative.

The scribes appear only for an instant (v. 14). They are arguing. We are not told why they are in a dispute. From what we know elsewhere in the Jesus narrative, perhaps they are trying to sort out what kind of regulation had been violated and who was responsible for the seizure of the boy. In the Gospel narratives the scribes stereotypically represent a quid pro quo world as they judge that such an "effect" has a "cause" in human conduct. The scribes seem to continue the work of Job's friends in the book of Job. Those friends, like the scribes, are determined to supervise a tight moral calculus. Perhaps the scribes are on to something important, but something that they themselves would not have discerned. We will return to their question, "Who caused this?" They are determined to keep the world morally symmetrical and explainable. The narrative has no interest in the question that I assume they were asking or in their motivation for that question.

The disciples are front and center in the narrative. As in so much of the Markan narrative, the disciples here are inept and ineffective, scarcely understanding who Jesus is and being unwilling and unable to sign on fully with him. In their response to the request that the father makes to Jesus, we learn that the disciples could not deal with "the spirit": "They could not do so" (v. 18). Much of the narrative turns on the inability of the disciples and their lack of faith. Jesus rebukes them for their lack of faith and is impatiently provoked by them: "You faithless generation, how much longer must I be among you? How much longer must I put up with you?" (v. 19). He parleys with the disciples who do not understand their own impotence (v. 28). His final response to them is a second rebuke to them: "This kind can come out only through prayer (and fasting)" (v. 29, au. trans.). The narrative focuses so much on the unfaith of the disciples that the mute boy is almost lost in the shuffle. But not quite!

JESUS SILENCES THE DEMON

In addition to this cast of characters there is Jesus. He evokes awe from the crowd (v. 15). He evokes hope in the father who looks past the impotent disciples to Jesus: "'I brought you my son'" (v. 17). The father had not intended to deal with the disciples but only with Jesus. He wanted to see the "real doctor," not an intern. But perhaps the disciples were to do the primary work only to have Jesus do the harder cases. Well, this is a harder case that the disciples could not manage. Jesus engages the disciples with a stunning reprimand. Jesus is at the center of the narrative, and with the exception of the scribes whom he does not address, he engages each of the other characters. It may be, as we will see, that he keeps in purview the presumed question of the scribes: "Who caused this?" But he is never explicit about that question, though it is implied all through the narrative.

The pivot of the narrative concerns *the faith of the father*, faith enough to bring the boy to speech, and *the unfaith of the disciples*. Jesus conducts an intake interview with the father about the son: "'How long has this been happening to him?'" (v. 21). The father responds, providing the required data, but ends with a passionate petition: "'From childhood. It has often cast him into the fire and into the water, to destroy him; but if you are able to do anything, have pity on us and help us'" (vv. 21–22).

Jesus and the father have an exchange about being "able," about having power, about mastering the destructive spirit. The father is eager but tentative: "'If you are able. . . .'" Jesus' magisterial response to the father wipes away any tentativeness on the father's part. Indeed, his response to the father is, in scope and key, well beyond the immediacy of the father: "'All things can be done for the one who believes'" (v. 23). Jesus' response is not unlike the one Jesus will make to Peter in the next chapter of Mark: "'For mortals it is impossible, but not for God; for God all things are possible'" (Mark 10:27).

To be sure, the two responses are different in their articulation. In our narrative the "possibility" is up to the person of faith. In the next chapter the "possibility" is only up to God. But it comes to the same point. Jesus apparently alludes all the way back to Genesis 18 where Abraham and Sarah in their old age are promised a son and an heir. Their response in that narrative is one of skepticism. Their skepticism, however, is met with a rhetorical question by the visitor(s): "'Is anything impossible for God?'" (Gen. 18:14; au. trans.).

The narrative sequence of the Bible has been at work on that question all through the generations. And now the question is posed again by the father and his needy son. In our narrative and in the narrative in chapter 10,

Jesus answers, "'All things can be done'" (9:23) and "'For God all things are possible'" (10:27). It is possible for the boy to be healed and restored. It is possible; but *God must be at work,* and *there must be faith.* Jesus does not ask the father to have the capacity to emancipate his son. He says only that it "'can be done,'" suggesting that Jesus can do it if the father trusts. The father, in his honesty, asserts his own ambiguity (v. 24). But his honesty is enough for Jesus, who promptly asserts his power toward the boy:

> "You spirit that keeps this boy from speaking and hearing, I command you, come out of him, and never enter him again!" After crying out and convulsing him terribly, it came out, and the boy was like a corpse, so that most of them said, "He is dead." (v. 25-26)

The father had sufficient faith to unleash the power of Jesus, which is the power of God. The news is that the spirit came out in obedience to Jesus; that spirit is now robbed of power to silence the boy. The act bears witness not only to *the adequate faith of the father* but to *the lordly capacity of Jesus.* All this is in contrast to the shabby unfaith of the disciples who could do nothing.

... the spirit came out in obedience
to Jesus; that spirit is now robbed
of power to silence the boy.

And then, with attentiveness to the corpse-like boy, "Jesus took him by the hand and lifted him up, and he was able to stand" (v. 27). The boy is healed and freed. Jesus is glorified. The boy becomes an occasion for the display of the capacity of Jesus to restore. Just to be sure we do not miss the point, note that the phrase "lifted him up" attests to an Easter resurrection. We are not told that the boy can speak. But he can stand. He can be a man, a lively human person. He is on the receiving end of restoration. He is raised up! He is restored to the fullness of life that had been denied him. The silence imposed by the spirit is broken by the restorative power of Jesus! The boy could break out in doxology at any moment.

WHO CAUSED THIS?

I want now to return to the question about which I assume the scribes were arguing (v. 14): Who caused this? Whose conduct evoked this crisis in the boy? Whose action caused this boy to be mute? The question assumes that such a "spirit" is not an accident or an arbitrary presence but that it has been dispatched in response to a willful intent. I take my clue in answering this scribal question from a sermon I heard by Dr. Michael Brandon McCormack.[1] It was a sermon preached at the summer conference of the Children's Defense Fund at Proctor Farm. McCormack is an African American professor who was speaking to a mostly African American congregation who got his point very quickly. McCormack took the "muteness" of the boy in our narrative as a figure for the "muteness" to which African Americans have been subjected and reduced in U.S. society. The image of muteness (silence!) meant for McCormack (and for us who listened) the *actions, attitudes, and policies of white racism* that have robbed African Americans of their capacity to speak, or live, or grow in their own future. Thus an African American, for all too long, could not speak until spoken to, could not look a white person directly in the eye,

---

Thus the boy, in twenty-first-century African American interpretation, has become a stand-in for the debilitating, paralyzing power of racism to reduce African Americans to see themselves as less than fully first-class human persons.

---

could not stay in town after dark, could not remain on a sidewalk where a white person wanted to walk, could not vote, could not enjoy the freedoms of American democracy, and could not benefit from the wealth of American capitalism . . . in sum, "Could not!" This long-term assault on African Americans in our society, so McCormack saw and said, was caused by the "spirit" of racism in all of its violent power, a spirit that robbed too many for too long of speech and of life. It is not a far stretch from the outcomes of the "spirit" of racism to imagine being cast into "the fire and into the water" to be destroyed (v. 22), to be reduced to foaming, grinding, and becoming rigid with fear (v. 18). I find McCormack's reading of this text powerfully compelling. Thus the boy, in twenty-first-century African American interpretation, has become a stand-in for the debilitating, paralyzing power of racism to reduce

African Americans to see themselves as less than fully first-class human persons. It is for good reason that the boy turns up in our society as "boy," a dismissive slander against African American men. It requires a powerful counterforce to overcome the debilitating power of racism in order for there to be restoration to new life and new speech.

If we read backward from McCormack's compelling interpretation to the time of Jesus, we may receive an answer to the scribal question. The boy is not undone by his sin nor by the sin of his father. The boy is ruthlessly reduced to silence by the imposing order of authoritarian religion, by the imperial requirement of Rome, by the pressure to conform, by the lack of freedom to embrace emancipated humanness. We cannot, I judge, know much about that first-century circumstance, but we know more about the twenty-first-century racism as our venue for such assaults on the vulnerable. The boy perhaps had had his imagination colonized by a dominant power so that he had no alternative to imposed disability. The wonder is that the father, like many wise African Americans, did not concede that it had to be this way for his son. He believed, not unlike William Barber among us now, that it could be otherwise.[2] No wonder he said, "Help my unbelief." He had perforce to host unbelief about the future because the power of paralysis seemed so formidable. But he also said, "I believe." He trusted in the capacity for new possibility. It is no wonder that he lived in the same profound ambiguity in which many honest people find themselves.

THE NEED TO BELIEVE

We may then understand why the disciples could not do the emancipatory work that the boy required and that the father requested. It is because the disciples were "faithless." The disciples did not believe an alternative was possible because they were profoundly inured into the dominant social habits of the day. In our day that would mean the dominant social habits of racism that continue with such power. The disciples could not believe in, trust in, or imagine anything beyond the dominant power arrangements, and so they were reduced to impotence.

Prayer is a refusal to settle for what is.

Jesus gives a clue about his transformative capacity. Such capacity comes only with prayer (v. 28). Prayer is an act of hope. It is an act of asking which trusts that new gifts can and will be given that will override present circumstance:

> Prayer indicates that the individuals involved have faith in God's power to bring about the requested outcome.[3]

Prayer is a refusal to settle for what is. But this is real prayer, down and dirty. It is not nice church prayer that refuses to ask anything because we mostly do not believe that prayers are heard or answered. Jesus ups the ante even more by adding "and fasting." The manuscript evidence for this last phrase in verse 28 is ambiguous, and translators commonly refuse to include it.

If, however, we let "fasting" stand in the text as some suggest, we may consider it to be an abstention from the seductions of dominant culture. For that reason, Jesus, in the previous chapter, has warned his disciples: "'Beware of the yeast of the Pharisees and the yeast of Herod'" (Mark 8:15).

The narrative suggests that the "one loaf" (which is Jesus in the Eucharist) is sufficient (8:14). To eat otherwise is to be compromised and left powerless for any alternative. Indeed, Mark can tell us that the disciples "did not understand about the loaves" (6:52). They did not understand about being nourished only by the broken bread of life and refusing all other forms of nourishment on offer. Behind the instruction of Jesus, moreover, we have the narrative of Daniel (1:8), who refused the rich food of the empire:

> But Daniel resolved that he would not defile himself with the royal rations of food and wine; so he asked the palace master to allow him not to defile himself.

Daniel then petitioned the guard whom the palace master had appointed over him (1:12):

> Please test your servants for ten days. Let us be given vegetables to eat and water to drink.

To be "defiled" by empire is to be robbed of a distinct identity that permits freedom against dominant culture. "Fasting" as alert abstention may be the order of the day that will make the asking of prayers more serious and compelling. The disciples knew none of this. They are of little faith, little prayer, and little fasting.

As a result, the boy, under their regime, remained as he had been, unable to speak.

JESUS BREAKS SILENCE

But not so with Jesus! Because Jesus was singularly committed to the rule of God, he was seen to embody that rule. He was indeed intimate with his heavenly Father (through prayer), and he surely distanced himself from the seductions of Rome and from the Jewish collusion with Rome (by fasting). He was thereby a free agent filled with transformative power.

The outcome of his enactment of power in this narrative is that the boy is "able to stand" (v. 27). He is no longer dashed down, foaming, grinding his teeth, and rigid. He is no longer immobilized by fear. He is no longer reduced to a hopeless, shabby, powerless, left-behind nobody because the coercive power of that spirit no longer holds sway. That coercive power has been overcome by the emancipatory power of God embodied and enacted by Jesus. For that reason, his father's hope is vindicated. His petition is justified, and his insistence rewarded.

It is quite remarkable that while Jesus reprimands his disciples, his engagement with them suggests that he believes that the disciples could yet be capable of transformative, emancipatory action. He believes that by the disciplines of *prayer* (holding fast to God) and *fasting* (refusing the seductions of dominant culture) the disciples could share in his transformative work. Without those disciples, however, no transformative power will be available, and the boy (and many like him) will be left in silent, hopeless circumstance.

The contest over the boy's body is now complete. It is no wonder that Luke, in his version of this story, can conclude, "And all were astounded at the greatness of God" (Luke 9:43). The small-minded ideology of domination did not know about the greatness of God. That small-mindedness would apply in our Markan narrative not only to the disciples but likewise to the scribes. The crowd had a better clue. The crowd was "overcome with awe" (9:15). Every time God's power is mobilized for emancipation and alternative, we may be overcome with awe. Indeed we may participate in such awe-evoking, transformative action, for it is all around us: many long-silenced people, like the boy, are coming to speech. They will not be silenced again by the power that works to destroy them. Jesus is offered in this text as the decisive antidote to the boy's muteness. Indeed, Jesus is the antidote, so the narrative attests, to the silence imposed everywhere on the earth. Now the crowd knows. The "spirit" was dispatched by coercive power that aimed at control. But the grip of that spirit of silence is broken by the centrality of Jesus in the story. Indeed, the story of Jesus is an account of breaking the silence.

QUESTIONS FOR REFLECTION

1. Describe what this story is about in your own words. What part of the story most strikes you?
2. In your opinion, who caused the boy's silence, and what is the significance of that?

3. The author tells of Dr. Michael Brandon McCormack's comparing the demon who silenced the boy with the silencing spirit of racism that for centuries has robbed African Americans of speech and full life. Is that a helpful comparison for you? Why or why not?

4. What is the function of prayer in situations like this?

Chapter 6

THE CROWD AS SILENCER

When he heard that it was Jesus of
Nazareth, he began to shout out and say, "Jesus,
Son of David, have mercy on me!" Many sternly
ordered him to be quiet, but he cried out even more
loudly, "Son of David, have mercy on me!"

—Mark 10:47–48

THE NARRATIVE OF A BLIND MAN FORCED TO BEG BEFORE
Jesus occurs in all three Synoptic Gospels (Matt.
20:29–34; Mark 10:46–52; Luke 18:35–43). Only in the
narrative of Mark is the blind man given a name, Bartimaeus. In Luke he remains unnamed, and in Matthew
there are two blind men who beg, both unnamed. The
action in our Markan passsage is clear and terse, and it
makes readily apparent the way in which the narrative
relates to our theme of silence.

BARTIMAEUS

Mark's telling of the story begins with a panoramic
view of the larger landscape of Jericho, the disciples,
and a large crowd, and then zooms in on the blind man

who begs. The large screen features not only Jesus and his disciples but also a large crowd of common folk who were eagerly attracted to Jesus. Our attention is drawn immediately to the blind man.

Blind Bartimaeus knew about Jesus of Nazareth. He had heard the popular stories that Jesus of Nazareth was a healer who was not domesticated by normal protocols and was not committed to custodial care for the sake of the status quo (see Mark 1:28). Prior to our narrative Jesus had accumulated ample narrative evidence that he possessed transformative power that moved well beyond the capacity of official institutions and agents. It is no wonder that Jesus drew a crowd. It is no wonder, moreover, that Bartimaeus sought him out.

Bartimaeus was a helpless man who depended on the generosity of neighbors. But neighborly generosity could do no more for him than custodial maintenance. Not surprisingly, he wanted more than that. He wanted restoration and rehabilitation, and he knew from long-suffering reality that custodial care, generous and indispensible as it might be, would never result in rehabilitation. He had to reach outside custodial care. He took that risk in his readiness to call out to Jesus. Maybe he had joined the crowd for just that purpose. Or maybe the excitement of the moment drew him out. He knew Jesus' name and identity. He accepted Jesus' popular pedigree as "Son of David," therefore the awaited, saving Messiah, and therefore the bearer of new historical, bodily possibility! Bartimaeus does not quibble about the correctness of that identity. It is good enough for him. He accepts as an act of hope.

He breaks the silence of his disability with an urgent imperative petition: "Have mercy on me!" (Mark 10:47). He does not decorate his need. He does not try to justify his imperative. He does not bargain, or bribe, or flatter, or offer motivation to Jesus. His imperative is the raw reality of his disabled life. With regard to his imperative petition, Meda Stamper has gone some effective distance in showing that in the Markan narratives many of the interactions between needy people and Jesus turn on the utterance of lament and thus echo the lament tradition of Israel that we know in the book of Psalms (see for example Pss. 6:2; 9:13).[1] Such an utterance, as in the ancient psalms, attests a need and requires a response that will relieve the need. In the ancient psalms most often, but not always, a good response is given. From that old tradition, Bartimaeus dares to hope and expect that his own lament may receive affirmative attention from Jesus, whom he takes to be the bearer of God's healing capacity.

THE CROWD AS SILENCERS

The interaction of the story, however, is not simply between Bartimaeus and Jesus, whom he addressed. We have already seen that Jesus is accompanied by a great crowd. And now that crowd actively enters the story of Bartimaeus: "Many sternly ordered him to be quiet" (v. 48). They are the silencers in an immense contest between *silence* and *the breaking of silence*. We are not told why the crowd ordered Bartimaeus to shut up. Perhaps they wanted to protect Jesus from such an annoyance. Perhaps they thought Jesus had more important matters with which to deal. Perhaps they knew that Bartimaeus was a recurring social pest and embarrassment, and they thought, "Not him again." Maybe he is like the kind of inconvenient pests who hang around the church. Perhaps they figured Jesus was too dangerous as a subversive to established order and did not want to witness a subversive and unauthorized healing. Perhaps they recognized that the title Bartimaeus had assigned Jesus, "Son of David," would evoke the hostility of Rome or, for that matter, the opposition of the guardians of Jewish tradition. We do not know; we only know that the crowd was readily mobilized for silence.

This is, for Mark, surely the same crowd (same word) that shows up before Pilate when at the festival the crowd had asked the Roman governor to function according to custom and release a prisoner (Mark 15:6–15). The governor wanted to release Jesus, whom he judged to be innocent, yet he needed the permission of the crowd. He may have had imperial authority, but he faced political reality, and the crowd would not grant the governor the permission that he sought. The reason for the crowd's resistance to the release of Jesus, we are told, is that the religious authorities who were threatened by the inexplicable authority of Jesus (the chief priests) had "stirred up" the crowd.

The crowd was easily mobilized. Perhaps the crowd, in its wisdom, knew that the release of Jesus would give this dangerous Jesus room to act, which would in turn evoke imperial hostility. In any case, the crowd, in this scene, following reactionary priestly leadership, voted for the status quo. We see the crowd before Pilate with its insistence:

> Pilate spoke to them again, "Then what do you wish me to do with the man you call the King of the Jews?" They shouted back, "Crucify him!" Pilate asked them, "Why, what evil has he done?" And they shouted all the more, "Crucify him!" (Mark 15:12–13)

That scene invites us to imagine that in the Bartimaeus narrative it is the same crowd that was readily mobilized against the petitionary summon to Jesus. In the scene with Pilate, they wanted Jesus permanently silenced. Now in our narrative, they wanted Bartimaeus silenced, because he might evoke transformative trouble.

The crowd, in its uncritical political engagement, is not always discerning about new possibility that comes with risk and often votes in fear for the status quo.

Apparently, Jesus did not hear Bartimaeus's cry for mercy when he first broke the silence. Perhaps his voice was drowned out by the crowd noise. There is more than one way to silence an unwelcome voice. It would have been possible for the narrative to end there. The crowd might have prevailed, as it often does. Bartimaeus could have settled in resignation about his poverty-stricken disability. He might have surrendered to the silence and left the world unchanged. That is what the crowd hoped for. The crowd, in its uncritical political engagement, is not always discerning about new possibility that comes with risk and often votes in fear for the status quo.

BARTIMAEUS PERSISTS

The story does not end with the intimidation of the crowd; if it ended there, we would not have the narrative. The wonder of the narrative is that Bartimaeus did not settle for resignation. He did not permit the silencers to win. He must have recognized that his present state was not "normal" for him, even though the crowd wished it to be his normal. The crowd always has a stake in pretending that the "abnormal" (in this case, being blind and begging) is "normal," for such a recharacterization of the abnormal as normal precludes some from full socioeconomic, political functioning. It would have been easy enough for Bartimaeus to conclude that his current situation, unbearable as it was, was to be his normal to perpetuity. The crowd encouraged him in despair, because greater expectation is unsettling for all parties.

Thus Bartimaeus continues the story by way of his courage and his resolve. His first breaking of the silence did not succeed. His attempt was defeated by the crowd, and Jesus did not hear him. But he makes a second, greater effort to break the silence. His second effort is very much like his first effort: "'Son of David, have mercy on me!'" (v. 48).

This time he does not name the name of Jesus but moves directly to the royal, messianic pedigree that had been assigned to Jesus. It is that identity of Jesus that gives ground for his alternative future. Again he summons the "Son of David." Again he issues his urgent petition. Again he offers no bribe, bargain, flattery, or motivation for Jesus, only the honest, raw need of body. It is all "again," a second time like the first time.

Except this second time he cried out "even more loudly" (v. 48). He knew, in the face of the crowd, that a vigorous, resolved voice is required to break the silence that has the sanction of both the authorities and the crowd. We have seen in our own day in so many liberation struggles that the first cry for mercy does not succeed. The silencers are powerful and determined. Among us the silencers are the powerful, who have a stake in the status quo and do not mind some poverty-stricken disability, and those who collude with the powerful, often unwittingly.[2] The work of silencing, like that of this crowd, is variously by slogan, by intimidation, by deception, or by restrictive legislation. Emancipation does not succeed most often in a one-shot effort. More is required. Bartimaeus knew that, and he makes a second effort . . . "even more loudly"!

JESUS CALLS, BARTIMAEUS JUMPS

"More loudly" worked, as it often does. Jesus hears the cry of Bartimaeus and immediately wants to see him. He responds without hesitation to his petition for mercy. Alan Culpepper sees that in verse 49 the term "call" is used three times: Jesus *called* him; they *called* him. They said to Bartimaeus, "He is *calling* you."[3] The repeated verb may be only a summons to an encounter, but it may also be a call to faith and discipleship. The blind man is being recruited to the Jesus movement. We are told then that "they" relayed the message to the blind man. Bartimaeus himself was not close enough to Jesus to hear his welcome. He was lost in the shuffle of the crowd. He required others to tell him of Jesus' response to him. We are not told who "they" are, perhaps Jesus' disciples or perhaps members of the crowd. If they are the latter, they may be the very ones who tried to silence Bartimaeus. But even if that is their identity, they are promptly responsive to Jesus' invitation to Bartimaeus. They encouraged Bartimaeus. They issued two quick imperatives to him:

"Take heart!" They encouraged blind Bartimaeus not to miss his chance but to respond quickly and hopefully to Jesus' invitation. Their imperative suggests that they recognized that Bartimaeus may have almost given up hope. But not quite!

"Get up!" Get moving! Do not miss your chance. Bartimaeus still has to make the first move. He has to initiate action that will become his restoration.

Bartimaeus accepts the urging of the crowd. He throws off his cloak that he had spread in order to receive alms. He left it behind the way folk do when they are called to Jesus, whether fishing nets or tax tables or their fathers. He will travel light in his hope-filled move.

He jumped up. He is ready! No doubt his eagerness concerns his prospect for healing and restoration. Beyond that, however, his immediately energetic response may suggest his readiness to sign on with Jesus because he already trusts that Jesus is the Lord of mercy.

SIGHT IS RESTORED

When Bartimaeus finally moves through the crowd to get to Jesus, the encounter is terse. Jesus offers only one question in his "intake interview." Surely he could have guessed what Bartimaeus wanted and hoped for. But he required Bartimaeus to verbalize his need, a verbalization that amounts to an act of uncommon hope. He has come to Jesus with the expectation that he can and will be healed. Thus he answers Jesus' question tersely and precisely: "'My teacher, let me see again'" (v. 51).[4] That is all. He addresses Jesus as "My teacher," the one who has the authority and the capacity to restore him.

Bartimaeus has screened out the crowd noise, whether the crowd is shushing him or encouraging him. Now there is only Jesus; he is in the presence of Jesus, and his breaking of the silence has gotten him there. In response to Bartimaeus, Jesus is equally terse. As is characteristic in these narratives of restoration, nothing is explained. The narrative evidences no need to know more, and no curiosity. It is enough to know and to see that interaction with Jesus is restorative. Jesus makes no claims for himself; he does not assert any authority. In fact he credits Bartimaeus's "faith" with the wonder of restoration, as though to fend off any hint that he has healed. It is as though the command of Jesus ("'Call him here'") and the presence of Jesus were enough of a trigger that permitted Bartimaeus to mobilize the restorative capacity of his own body. It could not have happened without Jesus!

The conclusion comes quickly: He saw . . . and he

followed. Notice that from the outset Bartimaeus had two disabilities. He was blind; now he can see. He was also poor, cast as a beggar, but the restoration of his sight says nothing about economic restoration, and we may suppose that he was as poor at the end of the narrative as he was at the outset. That, however, did not matter. He could continue to be poor because he now followed in the company of Jesus, the poor man from Nazareth.

TRANSFORMATIVE MERCY

Let us notice the pivot point of the narrative. Like all such narratives of restoration, this one turns in a dramatic moment from blindness to sight, from disability to restoration, from being "left behind" to being included in new company. Of course it is Jesus, as the narrative attests, who makes the decisive difference.

Jesus does not take the initiative. Jesus responds when he cried out "more loudly."

But Jesus can enter into the narrative only at the behest of the beggar. Bartimaeus must take the initiative. He must cry out. He must cry out more loudly. He must break the silence. He must violate the protocols that kept him in his place of disability. He must break the silence of the crowd of enforcers who wanted him to stay permanently in his place of disability. It was his breaking of the silence that propels the story. Jesus does not take the initiative. Jesus responds when Bartimaeus cried out "more loudly."

The narrative is a model and prototype for every emancipation. Any bondage of spirit or of body depends on colluding silence. Any emancipation depends on breaking the silence. Bartimaeus had, it turns out, the capacity to break the silence, a capacity of which he had been unaware. He had that capacity not because he was a believer in Jesus but because he paid attention to the truthful demands of his body. His body bore undeniable witness to him that his present state was not normal and was not right. It is this bodily insistence that becomes his ground for hope.

We may finally focus on the two-fold petition of Bartimaeus: "Have mercy on me!" The verb *mercy* (have mercy; *eleeo*), is closely linked to the noun *eleos* (mercy, pity) and to another noun, *eleamosune* (alms), all of which show up in our word *eleemosynary*. The play on "mercy/alms" is worth attention because they belong to the same semantic field, though they are very different. There is at present a growing and important focus on "almsgiving" in the Bible and in the early church as a means to salvation.[5] From the perspective of Reformation theology, such a claim sounds like "works righteousness." But a compelling case is readily made that in the early church movement almsgiving was regarded as a way to "store up treasure in heaven" (Matt. 6:19). It is important to notice, however, that as a beggar Bartimaeus had not sought "alms" from Jesus; he sought restoration of sight. The same distinction is evident in the narrative of Acts 3:1–10, in which the lame beggar asked Peter and John for alms. Peter responded,

> "I have no silver or gold, but what I have I give you; in the name of Jesus Christ of Nazareth, stand up and walk." (Acts 3:6)

Alms, that is, many ministries of charity, provide maintenance help and welcome custodial relief; the importance of such aid should not be understated. They do not, however, in themselves provide any chance for transformation. Peter's response is an indication that the earliest "poor church" had no resources for such relief. What it did have, however, was the capacity for restoration that was entrusted to it by Jesus:

> And he took him by the right hand and raised him up; and immediately his feet and ankles were made strong. Jumping up, he stood and began to walk, and he entered the temple with them, walking and leaping and praising God. (Acts 3:7–8)

The narrative of Bartimaeus, reinforced by the narrative of Acts 3, allows us to make an important distinction between *alms* and their custodial maintenance and *transformative mercy* that permits restoration. Bartimaeus did not seek alms from Jesus, and Jesus did not give him alms. Bartimaeus sought restoration, and Jesus evoked his restoration. Almsgiving might sustain the beggar in a world where the silence is never broken, but when the silence is broken, as in the case of Bartimaeus, something very different becomes possible.

The narrative of Bartimaeus ends tersely, and we never hear from him again. We may imagine, however, that his discipleship included teaching others that the way to restoration is by breaking the silence. Such a possibility, he knows, is on offer even in the face of the crowd that has such a large stake in the maintenance of silence for the sake of the status quo. He knows better. It is no wonder that he traveled with Jesus, the great silence breaker who broke the silence to offer new life.

QUESTIONS FOR REFLECTION

1. Why do you think the crowd tried to silence Bartimaeus?
2. Name some persistent Bartimaeuses you have known and how they were treated by the church.
3. What do you think of the point that Jesus didn't act until the man persisted and called out more loudly?
4. What is the difference between charity and transformative mercy? Name efforts you support in both categories.

Chapter 7

TRUTH SPEAKS TO POWER

*"In a certain city there was a judge
who neither feared God nor had respect for
people. In that city there was a widow who
kept coming to him and saying, 'Grant
me justice against my opponent.'"*

—Luke 18:2–3

JESUS TELLS THE DISCIPLES A PARABLE THAT ADDRESSES
two concerns. First, he intends that disciples should
"pray always" (18:1). Earlier in the Gospel of Luke he
had already given his disciples instruction in prayer.
That instruction included what we call the Lord's
Prayer, which pivots on asking (Luke 11:1–13). Prayer
is putting one's self in an acknowledged state of depen-
dence that relies on the gifts of God for life in the world.
Jesus assures that "'the heavenly Father will give the
Holy Spirit to those who ask'" (11:13). Theologian
Karl Barth said that prayer is indeed "simply asking."[1]
The parable is instruction in *asking.*

Jesus tells his disciples the story in Luke 18 so
that they do not "lose heart" (v. 1), that is, so that
they do not become discouraged and quit hoping. The

parable exhibits the relentlessness of refusing silence, the unwavering resolve to continue to speak and to ask. The inference is that the very act of prayer is a way to remain courageous, a way to resist resignation that would result in losing heart. The antidote to such defeat is the act of prayer, so prayer has an instrumental purpose. In this introduction Jesus does not assure the disciples that prayers are answered but only that the act of prayer is itself an act of resistance against discouragement and defeat.

The parable exhibits the relentlessness of refusing silence, the unwavering resolve to continue to speak and to ask.

Thus Jesus establishes a direct connection between *prayer* and not *losing heart*. The negative inference is that the disciples who do not "pray always," that is, stay linked to God in asking, will, sooner or later, "lose heart." Disciples do not have sufficient resources on their own to sustain a life of obedience but instead depend on God's continuing gifts in response to continual asking.

THE JUDGE AND THE WIDOW

As a master storyteller Jesus quickly invites his listening disciples into a freighted interaction. The interaction could happen anywhere: "In a certain city . . ." (v. 2). It features a judge and a widow. The judge is portrayed as cynical and indifferent; he "neither feared God nor had respect for people." Anything can happen in a parable, but we should not fail to notice that the parable permits this judge to be a stand-in for God, to whom petitions must be addressed. Of course a parable allows distance as well as identity, and we need not draw the connection of judge and God too closely. Nevertheless, if we track the parable, we may have a glance at a God who is indifferent and unresponsive.

The widow, on the other hand, is a recipient of injustice. Well, of course she was! In a patriarchal society widows are sure to be victimized because they have no male advocate. It is for this reason that the Torah repeatedly summons ancient Israel to care for widows (along with orphans and immigrants, the two other classes of patriarchal victims). The widow is resourceless. Again we should notice the implied parallel, even as we acknowledge that the parable allows distance as well as identity. We should not fail to notice that the parable presents the widow as a stand-in for the disciples, for in the rough and tumble of power the disciples are like the widow, powerless and vulnerable.

Thus the stage is set for a transaction between a cynical, indifferent judge and a resourceless widow who has been victimized. The alert listener is free to compute this as a transaction between a God who has gifts to give but who is indifferent about need and disciples who depend on these gifts in a world of jeopardy. The interaction between the judge and the widow is an asymmetrical one. But perhaps that is the point. The act of prayer is an asymmetrical one between a God who is addressed but perhaps not responsive and disciples who are needy and resourceless. And Jesus urges his disciples, "Stay active in this transaction, for staying active in this transaction will fend off despair."

BREAKING THE SILENCE
OF CONFORMITY

The interaction between the imperious judge and the needy widow is in three parts. First, the widow addresses the judge with an imperative: "'Grant me justice'" (v. 3). In the context of the story, it is a remarkable statement. No one would have expected a widow to speak up in court. No one would have thought the widow had justice on her horizon, or any sense of legitimate entitlement. Her bid for justice constitutes a recognition that the cards have been stacked against her and she has been exploited. In a patriarchal society such exploitation of a widow would have been business as usual, and she would have expected nothing other than that. But she does! She breaks the silence of conformity. She speaks out against the miscarriage of justice that would have seemed normal and routine in a patriarchal society. Indeed, we might imagine that some saw her bid as uppity. She filed a case in court that called into question what was taken for normal. She breaks the silence of conformity not only once, but she "kept coming" to the judge, speaking up repeatedly in court, perhaps regularly filing new claims and making new charges. It is no wonder that she is popularly labeled as "importunate" (au. trans.), a fancy term that means to "nag," or more respectably, to "urge irksomely." We can imagine that every time she showed up at the court, the clerks there all groaned because they knew what she wanted and they knew how it would turn out. She filed claims "always," as Jesus urged his disciples to "pray always."

We can imagine that every time she showed up at the court, the clerks there all groaned because they knew what she wanted and they knew how it would turn out. She filed claims "always," as Jesus urged his disciples to "pray always."

Second, the judge was unresponsive to her bid: "For a while he refused" (v. 4). He had no time for her claim. Likely he found some technical objection, some procedure that she did not carefully follow. She could not get a hearing from the judge. Of course it is like that in prayer because when we "pray always," we sometimes get a refusal because God is not an automaton of response, even as the judge had a dozen reasons for refusing her case.

But third, the judge relents, because her "urging irksomely" became too much for the judge to bear:

> "'Though I have no fear of God and no respect for anyone, yet because this widow keeps bothering me, I will grant her justice, so that she may not wear me out by continually coming.'" (v. 4)

This all happened "later." We are not told how much later, but it is after "for a while." The indifference of the judge, while long-lasting, did not and could not last as long as the urgent resolve of the widow. The judge, in his self-definition, confirms that he has no fear of God and no respect for anyone. As he knew, judges in their court rooms are as "gods" who are not called to account by anyone. They may be variously unresponsive or irresponsible or just quirky. We see it all the time. The judge has no interest in hearing the widow's case, no interest in her petition for justice. But finally she, by her continuing to speak out and break the silence of normal patriarchal protocols, prevails. She wears him out. NRSV adds as a note: "so that she may not finally come and slap me in the face." Her pesky resolve was indeed a slap in the face to the dignity of this judge who would not want to be exposed to such verbal harassment as her endless petition constituted. Thus by her refusal to be silent she got justice from a judge who never intended her to have justice. The widow beat the judge! Need overcame imperiousness. The truth of the widow's situation overwhelmed the imperious power of the court. Justice prevailed because she broke the silence and resolutely continued to break that silence.

WEAR GOD OUT IN PRAYER

In verse 6 Jesus steps out of the parable to address the disciples whom he has been instructing. He urges that the concession speech by the judge is what should be heeded. The judge had ruled for the widow because she had worn him out. That is the core of Jesus' instruction: Wear God out in prayer!

This counsel is followed by two questions with implied answers. First, "'Will not God grant justice to his chosen ones who cry to him day and night?'"

(v. 7). The answer is "Yes," yes God will! Yes, God will grant justice to "his chosen ones," the disciples who persist in their cry that voices both the urgency of pain and the formality of legal claim. That is the ground for "Pray always," because the God addressed in such urgent prayer finally will answer and give justice. Such an answer, however, depends on praying "always."

Second, Jesus asks the disciples, "'Will he delay long in helping them?'" (v. 7). No, there will be no long delay. God will give justice "quickly." I suppose that in the parable "quickly" is computed as "later," though we are not told how much later. These two questions look back to the introductory verse before the parable had begun. The insistent admonition is "Pray always and don't lose heart." The two questions in verse 7 with their implied answers are an assurance that praying "always" will bring justice "quickly." The introductory verses of the parable are an access point; the verse makes clear that a bid for justice from God requires breaking the silence of conventional protocol and dissenting. Even the power of God will not and cannot finally resist the bodily truth of the widow. It is conventional to assume that power in the world, even the power of God, does not need to answer to truth. But the parable tells otherwise and contradicts conventional assumptions. In the parable such power finally cannot resist the truth. An inkling of this claim is voiced in the Civil War verse of James Russell Lowell:

> Though the cause of evil proper,
> *Yet* the truth alone is strong:
> Though her portion be the scaffold,
> And upon the throne be wrong.

Yet that scaffold sways the future,
And behind the dim unknown,
Standeth God within the shadow,
Keeping watch above his own.[2]

Truth is on the scaffold, about to be executed. The poem's final stanza is introduced by "Yet" (that reiterates the "yet" of the preceding verse), which contradicts usual assumptions. This "yet" is a belated echo of the "yet" of verse 5 in the parable. In both cases "yet" tells otherwise and disrupts usual thinking. In the parable the "yet" allows that the capricious judge must give in to the resolve of the widow. In Lowell's poem the "yet" insists that the "execution of truth" is not the end of the story. God protects "his own," who in the parable is the insistent widow and in the text are the disciples as "his chosen ones" who are being instructed. God finally keeps watch for "his own," even against the predatory forces that govern by silence.

FAITH

The final verse of the parable text addresses the prospect of ultimate hope for the coming of "the Son of Man" (v. 8). The question posed in the verse is not about "the Lord's return" or the "Second Coming." It is rather about finding faith. In this context, faith consists in the resolve to seek justice. Faith is both the conviction that

---

Faith is both the conviction that
justice can be accomplished and
the refusal to accept injustice.

---

justice can be accomplished and the refusal to accept injustice. Thus in the parable the widow is an embodiment of profound, radical faith. Against all odds, against the silence of normalcy, she never doubted that justice could be had. Thus John Donahue can conclude about the parable:

> Luke understands continual prayer not simply as passive waiting but as the active quest for justice.[3]

Had she not had faith, the widow would have ceased to cry out. Had the disciples not had faith, they would not have prayed "always." Had they not prayed always, they would have lost heart. Thus the final verse is a crucial reflection on the company of Jesus and what it means to be in his company, perhaps a great hope or perhaps a great honesty about the reality of losing heart. What is clear is that faith is not a cognitive or creedal matter. It is rather a deep conviction that justice on the ground can be acquired, but it requires the breaking of silence before every indifferent judge, on earth and in heaven.

JUBILEE

We may usefully reflect on the relationship of this instruction about prayer with the "Lord's Prayer" of Luke 11:2–4. When we move from this destabilizing parable to the familiar prayer, we get more concern for justice. Sharon Ringe has gone so far as to suggest that the Lord's Prayer "can legitimately be called a jubilee prayer, that is, a prayer that God's Jubilee will come soon."[4]

The Jubilee, characterized in Leviticus 25 and anticipated in Isaiah 61:1 (on which see the quote in Luke 4:18–19), provided for the forgiveness of debts, the restoration to the land, and rest for the land. The diminishment of land and people results from relentless predation that ends in hopeless indebtedness, to which the Jubilee provided relief according to the Torah of God. Thus we may propose that the "justice" sought in the parable is, for the widow and for her hopelessly indebted neighbors, a petition that the Jubilee be enacted, that debts be forgiven, and that socioeconomic restoration for the "left behind" be implemented. In the parable the judge grants justice, and we may imagine that his act was indeed a cancellation of debts that permitted restoration of the widow to a viable life.

Read this way, the two prayers—the Lord's Prayer and the relentless petition of the widow—concern the enactment of Jubilee. The "faith" sought by the Son of Man is the conviction that the Jubilee is possible and will be enacted, for it is only debt cancellation that opens historical possibility for the hopelessly indebted. The breaking of silence by the widow—and by the church when it prays the Lord's Prayer—is an act of vigorous faith that the Jubilee may yet come about. Such a this-world action in the political economy is of course an outrageous expectation, but that is the intent of both prayers. Such an expectation, however, is congruent with the recurring accent on economic justice in Luke, an accent introduced by Luke already in the initial Song of Mary:

"He has filled the hungry with good things,
    and send the rich away empty."
                                    (Luke 1:53)

In "normal" politics, Jubilee is not possible. But the silence of normalcy (the normalcy of hopeless indebtedness) can be broken! Thus David Graeber, in his masterful study of the long, hopeless history of debt, ends his historical review with the judgment that it is only Jubilee and debt cancellation that make any societal future possible.[5] In drawing such a conclusion, Graeber of course echoes the tradition of Moses and of Jesus, and stands alongside the widow in her relentless cry.

LUKE ECHOES THE ELISHA STORY

We may conclude that this odd parable (offered only in Luke) is reflective of Israel's memory of Elijah and Elisha, who were quite practical performers of something like Jubilee.[6] More specifically, Elisha had ministered to a "wealthy women" by restoring her son who had died (2 Kgs. 4:8–37). Later on this same woman had relocated due to a famine and had been gone from her property for seven years (2 Kgs. 8:1–2). During that time her property had been assigned to others, surely the way the property of an absent woman would have been handled. When she returned home after the famine, her property was all lost to her. She is, however, a determined woman (that is, full of faith in the delivery of justice), and so she files an appeal (the text says she "cried out"[au.trans.]) to the king for the recovery of her lost property. The (nameless) king who hears her appeal is reported to be in the conversation with Elisha, who had done "great things" of restoration, including restoring the dead son of this woman. Perhaps it was the pressure and influence of Elisha that prompted the king to act when he received the petition of the woman. The king is reminded that Elisha had "restored" the son, and now the king has his chance to "restore" her property; he readily acts on her behalf:

> So the king appointed an official for her, saying, "Restore all that was hers, together with all the revenue of the fields from the day that she left the land until now." (2 Kgs. 8:6)

This was the king's "great thing" in the wake of Elisha. The king settles only this single case, but it is an instance of Jubilee for the woman whereby she is rehabilitated to her former life of well-being. I submit that our parable in Luke is an echo of the Elisha narrative.[7] In both texts the woman seeks justice and restoration, which are granted. In both cases the woman breaks the silence. In both cases the woman acts in faith, believing that justice is on offer for her.

The parable continues to be addressed to the church, the belated company of Jesus' disciples. The great temptation of the church is to accept the "normalcy" of this world with its penchant for hopeless indebtedness. Clearly faith is silence breaking with confidence that God's future—now to be performed—leads to correct the predatory practices against widows and other vulnerable persons. In the short run, the ones who administer the levers of power (like the judge or the king) need not heed the truth of these women.

Yet "later" it turns out otherwise, because she prayed "always" with pesky irksomeness.

QUESTIONS FOR REFLECTION

1. What does this parable teach about how to pray?
2. What does the parable teach about faith?
3. What is the silence that needs to be broken in this story?
4. Where do you see examples of this type of faith being practiced today?

Chapter 8

THE CHURCH AS A
SILENCING INSTITUTION

As in all the churches of the saints,
women should be silent in the churches.
For they are not permitted to speak, but
should be subordinate, as the law also says.
If there is anything they desire to know, let
them ask their husbands at home. For it is
shameful for a woman to speak in church.

—1 Cor. 14:33–35

THIS TEXT, SOMETHING OF AN ODDITY AND OF A SCANDAL
in the corpus of the Epistles, is a front-and-center study
for our theme of silence. It directly and unambiguously
prescribes the silencing of one element of the church
community by another segment of the community. It is
an oddity, but not singularly so, for the same prescription is commended elsewhere in the New Testament
Epistles:

> Let a woman learn in silence with full submission. I
> permit no woman to teach or to have authority over a
> man; she is to keep silent. (1 Tim. 2:12).

In a less direct way, other texts indicate the subordination
of women to men in the church (see Titus 2:15; 2 Pet. 3:1).

Not surprisingly a good many critical questions arise concerning our text in 1 Corinthians 14:34–35. We may wonder how this text belongs with others from Paul that clearly say otherwise. And if this text is not congruent with much of Paul, perhaps it is a later intrusion and does not come from Paul. But unless one is at work protecting Paul's reputation and legacy, this question does not matter greatly because the text is there in the epistle, and it has, over time, exercised immense pernicious influence in the church.

GENDER EQUITY IN PAUL'S COMMUNITY

We may begin reflecting more broadly with the evidence elsewhere from Paul concerning the relation of men and women in the church. First we should begin with the remarkable statement in Galatians 3:28 that is commonly taken to be a baptismal formula:

> There is no longer Jew or Greek, there is no longer slave or free, there is no longer male and female; for all of you are one in Christ.

To be "in Christ" is to be baptized into a different of set of social relationships:

> Our oneness in Christ overcomes and delegitimates the distinctions of race, social class, and gender that divided us when we were prisoners under the power of sin.[1]

Krister Stendahl, in a reference now lost to me, has observed that Paul's own work concerned Jews and Gentiles and only belatedly has the church gotten to the issue of slavery, and only in contemporary times, even more belatedly, has the church addressed the relation of "male and female." All of these social relationships, however, are inchoately present from the outset in the baptismal community, so that relationships in the new regime of Christ are radically changed from conventional practice.

Paul echoes the formula of Galatians 3:28 in 1 Corinthians 12:13:

> He [Paul] did not understand the baptismal formula to prescribe merely a spiritual equality before God in a way that had no social implications. Furthermore, the evidence on the other two issues (slavery and male/female relationships) is sufficiently ambiguous to suggest that Paul's vision did, in fact, destabilize traditional assumptions about power in a way that had practical implications in his communities.[2]

Paul reiterates the formula in 1 Corinthians 12:13, though that usage is absent in the third element of "male and female."

Second, the large claim made in the baptismal formula is evidently worked out in practice in the life of the early church. Thus Paul's Epistles indicate the readiness of Paul to share ministry with a variety of women whom he names. This roster includes Phoebe, Euodia, Syntyche, Apphia, and Prisca. The recurrence of such women in the Epistles of Paul leads Paul Sampley to this verdict:

> In the six undisputed letters apart from I Corinthians, no passage suggests any limitation on the role or function of women in the Pauline churches.[3]

There can be no doubt that in *its profession of faith* and in *its practice* the congregations planted by Paul were committed to gender equity that matched Paul's primary commitment to the equity of Jews and Gentiles in the church.

WHAT HAPPENS?

But then we are still left with our text, which unambiguously tells otherwise. Given the profession and practice indicated above, we are left with this prescription to the contrary. How shall we understand such a variance? At the outset we might judge that it is a long, hard step from sweeping profession to actual concrete practice. We have all experienced that in our own lives and in the life of the church. Thus Hayes is surely correct when he judges,

> Of course the practical outworking of this vision of the new creation remains the ongoing task of the church in history as we "eagerly wait for the hope of righteousness" (5:5).[4]

The key is "practical outworking" that must deal with well-established practices in society all around the church. It is, moreover, not unlikely that Paul himself had impulses from the traditional practice of female subordination, impulses reflected in the belated articulations of Ephesians 5:22–24 and Colossians 3:18–19. And if these letters are not from Paul, they are certainly linked to the circles in which he lived and worked.

It may be, as many scholars contend, that our verses are a later intrusion into the epistle. If that is the case, then the articulation of these verses may reflect a development of a more "institutional" way of thinking and organizing the community, a development often linked to the Pastoral Epistles (see glossary). Given such a development the early church may have been willing, as happens when movements become institutions, to compromise its most sweeping claims and to accommodate social reality and expectation. If we may allow for the lateness of our text, this suggests that derivative from Paul is a readiness to accommodate social resistance to equity, even in the name of Paul.

Given such a development the early church may have been willing, as happens when movements become institutions, to compromise its most sweeping claims and to accommodate social reality and expectation.

The best that can be made of our verses is that the early church operated in an honor/shame society. Perhaps in that frame of reference outspoken women were an embarrassment for their husbands, that is, they brought social shame on them. Thus it would follow that the silencing is to be practiced in order to honor the male members of the community.

However the practical issues may be parsed, the fact remains that our text evidences the act of silencing whereby the voices of women are silenced in a way that contradicts the church's baptismal profession and the practice of much of the church. As always with imposed silence, the protection of power and privilege proceeds without scruple in a worldly practice of domination.

SILENCING IS ALIVE AND WELL TODAY

Whatever may be our interpretation about the intention of this text in the early church in the orbit of Paul, the fact is that the text is there and has exercised an enormously pernicious influence in the life of the church. In appealing to this text in order to silence women in the church, there is no lingering over the question of Pauline authorship or concerning the slippage between profession and practice. The text rather has been treated as a flat absolute that seems obvious to those who have read and continue to read it uncritically. As a result, the practical outcome has been a long history of subordination of women in the church that has evoked hard struggle over the authorization of ordination for women and their empowerment in the church. For all that we know about the baptismal formula of Galatians 3:28, the struggle had not seen much success in the wider church until the middle or later part of the twentieth century. Institutions, even well-intentioned ones, are not readily open to the realignment of power and privilege. Indeed, a recent *New York Times* article told about a protest of Jewish women at the Wailing Wall in Jerusalem for equal rights and privileges for women who want to pray at the Wall. In the photo these protesting women are carrying Torah scrolls, making visible their claim to legitimacy at the Wall.[5] Prime Minister Netanyahu "accused the liberal Jewish women of causing 'unnecessary friction' and of 'the unilateral violation of the status quo of the Wailing Wall.'" Of course, it is no different in the church; when the silence is broken there is indeed a unilateral violation of the status quo, and reaction is often swift.

We may therefore reflect on the church as a silencing institution in which the claims of the gospel have been commonly violated for the sake of control and privilege. That silencing has concerned women, but the silencing for the same reason has been extended to many populations that constitute the "other" to white-male, Western domination.

The Roman Catholic Church, with its well-ordered hierarchy and its commitment to centralization, is able to sustain silencing in a quite formal way by the practice of excommunication or, as in the noted cases of Hans Kung and Leonardo Boff, the church is said to "silence" its teachers who violate the absolutes of the "magisterium." Those who are silenced of course are not made mute, but they are deauthorized and can claim no legitimacy in the church to which they have given their lives.

In 2016 Pope Francis (*even* Pope Francis) made clear, in the wake of an ecumenical meeting in Lund, Sweden, that the ordination of women would be prohibited forever.[6] It was a statement freighted with irony because it followed a celebration of reconciliation with Lutherans at the anniversary of the Reformation. Francis yet again appealed to the ludicrous, often-repeated reason that Jesus had had no female disciples. Of course that long-standing prohibition is deeply at risk because serious Catholics can read the Gospel texts other than the prohibition in our text. But the opinions of many

Catholics, as well as the "nuns on the bus," suggest that male domination may not have the last word, because the spirit may blow in other directions.

Other expressions of the Christian movement do not have the measured mechanics for silencing that belong more readily to a hierarchal church. But even sectarian movements in the church have the technique of "shunning," an effective social maneuver that reads people out of the community if they violate the norms. The silencing works well in such a maneuver.

Such churches, not unlike the Catholic reliance on nuns, have been willing to utilize the cheap labor of women as long as that labor did not make any claim to authority.

More conservative, evangelical church communities share a long tradition of being wounding institutions. Very often such wounding revolves around an authoritarian pastor who takes for himself a voice of absolutism that can determine who is in and who is out. Such authoritarian churches have long silenced women or have excluded women's voices in the teaching, pastoral office. Such churches, not unlike the Catholic reliance on nuns, have been willing to utilize the cheap labor of women as long as that labor did not make any claim to authority. The propensity to absolutism has been a ready tool for social control that has widely been in the service of racism and in the current struggle for the rights and legitimacy of homosexuals.

Given such absolutism such voices readily become equated with the truth of God.

The matter is slightly different in so-called progressive churches that profess to be all-inclusive and that prefer such slogans as "All are welcome." In such traditions (including my own United Church of Christ), however, the actual practice of silence is done through ideological purity so that voices to the contrary result in exclusion. In progressive tradition, it is not women who are silenced but many others are who do not submit to the "liberal absolutism."

I intend, by my comment on Catholics, sectarians, evangelical conservatives, and liberal progressives (with a glance at the struggle in Judaism) to suggest that in all parts of the church, readiness for silencing and wounding are alive and well. All of that, of course, cannot be blamed on our text. A review of such a propensity to silencing and wounding, however, does illuminate both why we have such a text in our canon and how such a text has continued to feed and legitimate that propensity.

There is no practical area in the life of the church in which reform is more urgent than in the church's propensity (in all of its manifestations) to silence. Such reform, like every moment of reform, means a return to the core claims of the gospel. In this case, it is the core claim of the baptismal formula of Galatians 3:28 concerning the third element of "male and female." As Stendhal observed, we are slowest about this third member of the triad.[7] As the church in reform draws closer to its core confession, it inescapably embraces its most radical vision that violates and contradicts conventional practice in its social context. What makes such reform difficult, moreover, is the fact that while we ponder the radical core claims of faith, we ourselves are variously enmeshed in conventional practices that are inimical to the gospel.

CHALLENGE ORIGINALISM

Finally, we are left with the text in 1 Corinthians 14:34–35. It is a prescriptive statement to which easy appeal can be made. Our society has lately been beset by an epidemic of "strict constructionism" that was famously championed by the late conservative Supreme Court Justice Anthony Scalia. Scalia's concern, of course, has been with the U.S. Constitution. In his reading, the original intent of the writers of the Constitution is the final word. It happened, of course, that Scalia's original intent always tilted in a conservative direction and most often agreed with his own conservative propensity. This doctrine of originalism was a backward look to a society the way it used to be or the way it wanted itself to be remembered.

That doctrine of originalism is in fact only another version of fundamentalism, in which the literal meaning of a text is taken without critical attentiveness to context. When the doctrine is applied to Scripture, a judgment about the silencing of women, uncritically and without context, can be taken as an absolute prescription. This is the conclusion about silencing women that has been operative in much of the church.

But of course fundamentalism (or originalism) in

both Constitution and Scripture is not sustainable pre-cisely because the human community is in process and under way. Such process requires that both the Con-stitution and the Bible be living documents that must always be reread afresh. And in fact at some level everyone accepts that reality, even if grudgingly. Thus, for example, almost no one believes any longer that African American persons (still very much indentured) are only three-fifths of a person, as the Constitution prescribes. Almost no one believes that homosexuals should be executed, as the Torah prescribes. We do rereadings of Constitution and Bible as circumstance requires, even if we do it grudgingly or if we do it without acknowledgment.

Thus our text on the silence of women in the church cannot be read as a flat absolute in the twenty-first century but must be read in context where criti-cal thought tells against any silly judgment that Jesus had only male disciples. For that matter Jesus had only Jewish disciples, not a single Italian, Pole, German, or Argentinian.

This rereading of the text requires freedom, cour-age, and imagination that move beyond originalism and strict constructionism to see what the elemental claims of the gospel might be in new circumstances. We may note three recent rereadings of the Bible, in each case concerned with gender, that illuminate the Bible as a living document.

In 1993 a group of women in the Presbyterian Church organized the Re-Imagining Conference for women in Minneapolis. The program featured an extended ros-ter of gifted feminist interpreters who variously explored fresh articulations of God, Jesus, creation, and the church from a reconsideration of Scripture. The conference was a spectacular success. But what followed by way of reaction was even more stunning. The conference evoked immense hostility among church people and many others who were scandalized by such an act by women and by the daring act of reinterpretation that challenged long-settled consensus. The "re" part of "re-imagining" and "reinterpretation" indicated that old conclusions would not be honored and old consensus would not prevail. Women's voices were indeed unleashed that broke the silence.

At about the same time, in 1992, a coalition was formed in the Presbyterian Church dubbed the More Light Churches Network. It was concerned with the rights of gays and lesbians. The More Light Church Network proposed to reinterpret Scripture and tradition in the church in a fresh and emancipatory way. The movement took its name from a phrase of John Robinson, the spiritual leader of the pilgrims who founded the Plymouth Colony. Robinson famously declared that "the Lord has more truth and light yet to break forth out of his holy word." Robinson was clear that Scripture as "God's word" continued to yield new revelatory truth, so that its truthfulness is not completed or exhausted in established readings. The Bible can do so because it is a venue for the Spirit. Specifically the network found that attention to Scripture will deliver news about the rights of gays and lesbians who had been long silenced and made invisible in the church. That "new light" of course disturbed and disrupted those who were committed to old patterns of silencing.

In a parallel development, my own church, the United Church of Christ, adopted the phrase "God Is Still Speaking." The phrase, with direct reference to the rights of gays and lesbians, intended to affirm that the old assumptions of the Bible about such persons were not true because God's spirit continues to live in the church in new and faithful ways.

All of these three emergents—*Re-imagining, More Light,* and *Still Speaking*—are evidence that the old silences are being broken. In each case, moreover, the gender issues are primary because the silencing of gays and lesbians is but the next step after silencing women. In each case, the insistence is that such silencing based on gender is no longer acceptable because the Spirit has led us elsewhere and otherwise.

The old pattern of silencing served old-time religion, and old-time religion is in the service of old-time politics of domination and old-time economics of privilege. Strict constructionism and originalism are always in the service of old-time religion, old-time economics, and old-time politics. The breaking of that silence for women and for many others depends on Re-imagining, More Light, and Still Speaking. It turns out that these emergent new readings place everything "old time" in jeopardy.

QUESTIONS FOR REFLECTION

1. How have you reconciled conflicting biblical texts about the role of women in the church previously? How has this chapter confirmed or challenged your previous thinking?

2. What do you think happened in biblical texts to make later writings go backwards in terms of inclusion of women? How does institutionalizing movements compromise more radical thinking?

3. Where else have you seen the modern church silence people on the margins?

4. How should the church challenge originalism?

GLOSSARY

BCE and CE. Before the Common Era and Common Era, often replacing BC/AD (before and after Christ). This is a practice that has developed in the scholarly world of biblical study where Jews and Christians work side by side. In that setting, and in our culture at large as it is now developing, Christian domination is not appropriate or accurate.

For most of the first three hundred years of the Christian movement, Christians were a very small minority who shared with the Jews the common belief in God and a refusal to bow before the Roman emperors or deities. Thus we began by sharing—it was a common era. It was only much later, in the fifteenth century, that the BC/AD symbols came into common use. And actually, it is only in the West and because of the economic/military domination of the West, that this calendar (BC/AD) is used. In many other parts of the world, different symbols are employed that are only secondarily "adjusted" to fit the calendar of the West.

Davidic line. Also called the House of David. Refers to David's descendants.

exile. In July, 586 BCE, Babylonian soldiers broke through Jerusalem's walls, ending a starvation siege that had lasted well over a year. They burned the city and Solomon's temple and took its king and many other leaders to Babylon as captives, leaving others to fend for themselves in the destroyed land. Many surrounding countries disappeared altogether when similar disasters befell them. But Judah did not. Instead, the time scholars most often call the "Babylonian exile" inspired religious leaders to revise parts of Scripture that had been passed down to them. It also sparked the writing of entirely new Scriptures and the revision of ideas about God, creation, and history. Much of what is called the Hebrew Scriptures or Old Testament was written, edited, and compiled during and after this national tragedy.

Pastoral Epistles. *Epistle* means letter. The Pastoral Epistles refer to the three letters Paul wrote to Timothy (1 and 2 Timothy) and Titus.

Torah. Often called the Pentateuch in English. It refers to the first five books of the Hebrew Scriptures, which Christians usually call the Old Testament.

YHWH. This name for God is often written "Yahweh," although it is four Hebrew consonants that spell the name. In Exodus 3 God tells Moses to tell the Israelites living as slaves in Egypt that God will liberate them from Pharaoh. Moses asks God what name Moses should use for God, and God says, "YHWH" (Exod. 3:14), often translated "I AM WHO I AM."

Zion. Originally an actual location in Jerusalem on the southeastern hill of the city that became David's capitol and later site of Solomon's Temple. Biblical writers and poets used the term in symbolic ways that do not distinguish the city, the temple, the monarchy and its political-military apparatus. Zion became the symbol for the faith of Israel in its future to be given by God.

NOTES

Introduction

1. Nina Siegal, "Dutch Politician Is Convicted of Inciting Discrimination, but Not Punished," *The New York Times*, December 10, 2016, A3.

2. Gerald T. Sheppard, "'Enemies' and the Politics of Prayer in the Book of Psalms," in *The Bible and the Politics of Exegesis*, ed. David Jobling et al. (Cleveland: Pilgrim Press, 1991), 81.

3. Lewis Hyde, *The Gift: Creativity and the Artist in the Modern World* (New York: Vintage Books, 2007), 218.

4. Ibid., 220.

Chapter 1: The Oppressed Break Silence

1. Pamela Constable, *Playing with Fire: Pakistan at War with Itself* (New York: Random House, 2011), 23–24.

2. Ibid., 24.

3. See Antonio Gramsci, quoted in Enrique Dussell, *Ethics of Liberation in the Age of Globalization and Exclusion* (Durham, NC: Duke University Press, 2013), 243.

4. Jon D. Levenson, *The Hebrew Bible, the Old Testament, and Historical Criticism* (Louisville, KY: Westminster John Knox Press, 1993) 127–59.

Chapter 3: Silence Kills

1. John Calvin, *Commentary on the Book of Psalms,* Volume 1 (Grand Rapids: Baker Book House, 1979), 530.

2. John Murray Cuddihy, in *The Ordeal of Civility: Freud, Marx, Levi-Strauss and the Jewish Struggle with Modernity* (New York: Delta Books, 1976), has probed in a helpful way the significance of Freud's Jewish legacy.

Chapter 4: Jesus Rudely Interrupted

1. Elisabeth Schüssler Fiorenza, *But She Said: Feminist Practices of Biblical Interpretation* (Boston: Beacon Press, 1992), 96–103. My discussion is greatly indebted to her reading of the narrative.

2. Ibid. 97.

Chapter 5: Casting Out Silence

1. Dr. McCormack teaches at the University of Louisville and at the Louisville Presbyterian Theological Seminary.

2. See William J. Barber II, *The Third Reconstruction: Moral Mondays, Fusion Politics, and the Rise of a New Justice Movement* (Boston: Beacon Press, 2016).

3. Pheme Perkins, *The Gospel of Mark*, MIB VIII (Nashville: Abingdon Press, 1995), 635.

Chapter 6: The Crowd as Silencer

1. Meda A. A. Stamper, "The Bad Things Shout Louder: Mark, Brueggemann, and the Life of Faith," *Imagination, Ideology, and Inspiration: Echoes of Brueggemann in a New Gen-*

eration, ed. Jonathan Kaplan and Robert Williamson (Hebrew Bible Monographs 72; Sheffield, UK: Sheffield Phoenix Press, 2015), 219–36.

2. See, for example, Thomas Frank, *What's the Matter with Kansas: How Conservatives Won the Heart of America* (New York: Henry Holt, 2005).

3. R. Alan Culpepper, *Mark* (Smyth & Helwys Commentary; Macon, GA: Smyth & Helwys, 2007), 354.

4. Ibid., 354–55.

5. I have found most helpful David J. Downs, *Alms: Charity, Reward, and Atonement in Early Christianity* (Waco, TX: Baylor University Press, 2016). Attention should also be given to Gary A. Anderson, *Charity: The Place of the Poor in the Biblical Tradition* (New Haven, CT: Yale University Press, 2013), and the magisterial work of Peter Brown, *Through the Eye of a Needle: Wealth, the Fall of Rome, and the Making of Christianity in the West 350–550 AD* (Princeton, NJ: Princeton University Press, 2011).

Chapter 7: Truth Speaks to Power

1. Karl Barth, *Church Dogmatics*, III/3, *The Doctrine of Creation* (Edinburgh: T. & T. Clark, 1960), 268.

2. James Russell Lowell's "Once to Every Man and Nation" was written in 1845 in the context of the national dispute concerning slavery that then erupted in the U.S. Civil War.

3. John R. Donahue, *The Gospel in Parable* ((Philadelphia: Fortress Press, 1988), 185.

4. Sharon H. Ringe, *Jesus, Liberation, and the Biblical Jubilee: Images for Ethics and Christology* (Overtures to Biblical Theology; Philadelphia: Fortress Press, 1985), 81–84.

5. David Graeber, *Debt: The First 5,000 Years* (Brooklyn, NY: Melville House, 2011).

6. See Thomas L. Brodie, *Proto-Luke: The Oldest Gospel Account: A Christ-Centered Synthesis of Old Testament History Modeled especially on the Elijah-Elisha Narrative* (Limerick, IE: Dominican Biblical Institute, 2006).

7. See Walter Brueggemann, "A Royal Miracle and Its

Nachleben," The Economy of Salvation: Essays in Honor of M. Douglas Meeks, ed. Jurgen Moltmann et al. (Eugene, OR: Cascade Books, 2015), 9–22.

Chapter 8: The Church as a Silencing Institution

1. Richard B. Hayes, "The Letter to the Galatians," NIB XI (Nashville: Abingdon Press, 2000), 279.

2. Ibid., 278.

3. J. Paul Sampley, "The First Letter to the Corinthians," NIB 10 (Nashville: Abingdon Press, 2002), 969, italics in the original.

4. Hayes, "The Letter to the Galatians," 279.

5. Isabel Kershner, "Netanyahu Criticizes American Jewish Leaders," *The New York Times*, November 3, 2016, A11.

6. "Pope Francis Says Ban on Female Priests Is Likely to Be Forever," *The New York Times* (November 2, 2016).

7. Krister Stendahl, oral communication to author.